Better Homes and Gardens®

QUILTS TO MAKE FOR KIDS

The Crafts Department at Better Homes and Gardens Books assembled this collection of projects for your crafting pleasure. Our staff is committed to providing you with clear and concise instructions so that you can complete each project. We guarantee your satisfaction with this book for as long as you own it. We welcome your comments and suggestions. Please address your correspondence to Better Homes and Gardens Book Crafts Department, 1716 Locust Street, LS-352X, Des Moines, IA 50336.

© Copyright 1991 by Meredith Corporation, Des Moines, Iowa.
All Rights Reserved. Printed in the United States of America.
First Edition. First Printing.
Library of Congress Catalog Card Number: 90-64100
ISBN: 0-696-01908-6 (hard cover)
ISBN: 0-696-01909-4 (trade paperback)

BETTER HOMES AND GARDENS® BOOKS

Vice President, Editorial Director: Elizabeth P. Rice
Art Director: Ernest Shelton
Managing Editor: David A. Kirchner
Project Editors: James D. Blume, Marsha Jahns
Project Managers: Liz Anderson,
    Jennifer Speer Ramundt, Angela K. Renkoski

Crafts Editor: Sara Jane Treinen
Senior Crafts Editors: Beverly Rivers, Patricia Wilens
Associate Crafts Editor: Nancy Reames

Associate Art Directors: Neoma Thomas,
    Linda Ford Vermie, Randall Yontz
Assistant Art Directors: Lynda Haupert,
    Harijs Priekulis, Tom Wegner
Graphic Designers: Mary Schlueter Bendgen,
    Michael Burns, Mick Schnepf
Art Production: Director, John Berg;
    Associate, Joe Heuer;
    Office Manager, Michaela Lester

President, Book Group: James F. Stack
Vice President, Retail Marketing: Jamie L. Martin
Vice President, Administrative Services: Rick Rundall

BETTER HOMES AND GARDENS® MAGAZINE
President, Magazine Group: James A. Autry
Editorial Director: Doris Eby

MEREDITH CORPORATION OFFICERS
Chairman of the Executive Committee: E. T. Meredith III
Chairman of the Board: Robert A. Burnett
President and Chief Executive Officer: Jack D. Rehm

Quilts to Make for Kids
Editor: Patricia Wilens
Photography Editor: Beverly Rivers
Contributing Editor: Lynette Jensen
Graphic Designer: Lynda Haupert
Project Manager: Angela K. Renkoski
Contributing Illustrator: Chris Neubauer
Contributing Writer: Sharon Novotne O'Keefe
Electronic Text Processor: Paula Forest

Cover project: See page 53.

CONTENTS

LULLABY AND GOOD NIGHT

♦ ♦ ♦

Baby soft and stitched with love, the enchanting quilts and accessories in this chapter go from sleepy time to playtime and on to a pram ride in the park. Charm fills the nursery with a bright wall hanging of whimsical motifs such as our appliquéd troupe of tumbling pandas that are sure to win smiles. These quilts offer many techniques—machine appliqué, quick piecing, stenciling—as well as traditional quiltmaking methods.

Inspired by one of a baby's first and favorite games, the Peekaboo Crib Quilt, *right,* is more than a toasty topper for your little one's bed. It is also a tote-along learning toy for happy play anywhere.

Nursery pretty in fresh pastels, this quilt scored high on our real-life kid test because it is stitched up with surprises. Centered in the quilt's 12 pieced blocks, simple appli-quéd shapes such as a heart, a balloon, an apple, and a kite hide behind fabric doors. Self-grip fasteners make it easy for tiny fingers to unlock each door.

The simple shapes may be appliquéd by hand or by machine, and the quilt may be tied or hand-stitched.

A crib-size charmer at 45x66 inches, it can be enlarged for a bigger bed. The blocks are joined with alternating setting squares and triangles in diagonal rows and edged in a double border.

Instructions begin on page 10.

LULLABY AND GOOD NIGHT

◆ ◆ ◆

Baby soft and stitched with love, the enchanting quilts and accessories in this chapter go from sleepy time to playtime and on to a pram ride in the park. Charm fills the nursery with a bright wall hanging of whimsical motifs such as our appliquéd troupe of tumbling pandas that are sure to win smiles. These quilts offer many techniques—machine appliqué, quick piecing, stenciling—as well as traditional quiltmaking methods.

Inspired by one of a baby's first and favorite games, the Peekaboo Crib Quilt, *right,* is more than a toasty topper for your little one's bed. It is also a tote-along learning toy for happy play anywhere.

Nursery pretty in fresh pastels, this quilt scored high on our real-life kid test because it is stitched up with surprises. Centered in the quilt's 12 pieced blocks, simple appliquéd shapes such as a heart, a balloon, an apple, and a kite hide behind fabric doors. Self-grip fasteners make it easy for tiny fingers to unlock each door.

The simple shapes may be appliquéd by hand or by machine, and the quilt may be tied or hand-stitched.

A crib-size charmer at 45x66 inches, it can be enlarged for a bigger bed. The blocks are joined with alternating setting squares and triangles in diagonal rows and edged in a double border.

Instructions begin on page 10.

CONTENTS

Yesterday's child surely dined in dainty bibs and snuggled under colorful comforters like this endearing duo. But, though the look is decidedly old-fashioned, today's products make these projects easy-care and easy to sew.

All dressed up in lacy edging and ribbons, the pretty bib, *above,* is made of washable cotton fabric, and its delicate floral design can be quilted by machine or by hand.

Instructions and a full-size pattern are on pages 13 and 14.

Cheery stenciled tulips bloom across this quick-to-sew crib quilt, *opposite.* Use washable fabric paints for stenciling the tulip blocks and leafy border design.

The instructions start on page 15 and include tips for making this quilt by hand appliqué.

6

Babies love lively colors, especially when they're combined with whimsical motifs that spark the imagination.

With a bold black-and-white checkerboard pattern, splashes of warm hues, and a just-for-fun theme, the Playful Pandas Quilt, *right,* makes an irresistible crib cover or an eye-catching focal point as a wall hanging. Teamed with the matching diaper bag, it is also a great take-along item for baby's outings.

The heartwarming troupe of somersaulting pandas is appliquéd around the edge of a center medallion.

Classic nine-patch squares are used for the checkerboard design in the center and on the borders; instructions include tips to make these by machine with quick strip piecing or by traditional methods.

The finished quilt measures approximately 51 inches square.

Roomy enough for diapers and baby supplies, the matching bag is lined and has a handy outer pocket. It measures approximately 19x22 inches.

Directions for both panda projects begin on page 18.

Peekaboo Crib Quilt

Shown on pages 4 and 5.

The finished crib quilt measures 45x66 inches. Each pieced block is 8 inches square.

MATERIALS
2 yards of print fabric for blocks, borders, and binding
1⅛ yards of muslin for windows and setting triangles
¾ yard *each* of blue dotted fabric for the inner border and peach striped fabric for the setting squares
⅛ yard *each* of yellow, pink, and purple fabrics for block piecing and appliqué
3 yards of backing fabric
54x75-inch piece of quilt batting
Twelve ½-inch-diameter self-grip fastening tape circles
Permanent-ink marking pen
¼ yard of paper-backed webbing for machine appliqué
Template material
Rotary cutter, mat, and ruler

INSTRUCTIONS
This quilt provides hours of delight for playful toddlers. A lined door, sewn into the seam, covers the appliquéd center of each of 12 blocks. The appliqué is revealed when the child lifts the door. This type of play helps kids learn to identify objects and colors.

The peekaboo blocks are set together with setting squares in diagonal rows. Each row is finished with muslin setting triangles.

Cutting the fabrics
Cut ten 4½x42-inch strips of the border print fabric; set aside six strips for the border.

Cut the remaining four strips of border print fabric into thirty-six

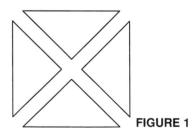

FIGURE 1

4½-inch squares. Set 12 squares aside for the peekaboo doors. Referring to Figure 1, *below,* cut the remaining squares in quarters diagonally for a total of 96 triangles.

Cut six 2¼x42-inch strips of the border fabric for binding.

For the setting squares, cut six 8½-inch squares of peach fabric.

Cut two 4½x42-inch strips of muslin; from these strips, cut twelve 4½-inch squares for the appliqué blocks.

For the setting triangles, cut three 13½-inch squares and two 9½-inch squares of muslin. Cut the three larger squares in quarters diagonally to obtain the 10 side triangles. Cut the smaller squares in half diagonally for the four corner triangles. *Note:* These triangles are slightly larger than necessary and will be trimmed before the borders are added.

For the border, cut six 2½x42-inch strips of blue dotted fabric.

From *each* of the yellow, pink, and purple fabrics, as well as the remaining blue dotted fabric, cut one 3¾x24-inch strip; cut each strip into six 3¾-inch squares. Cut all the squares in half diagonally to make 12 triangles of each fabric. Use the remaining scraps of fabric for the appliqués.

Divide the backing fabric into two 54-inch-long panels. Cut a 4½x54-inch strip from the side of one panel. Set the panels aside for the back; cut the 4½-inch-wide strip into twelve 4½-inch squares for the door linings.

Preparing fabrics for appliqué
The quilt shown was appliquéd by machine. Instructions are given for both hand- and machine-appliqué techniques. Do not apply fusible webbing to the appliqué fabrics for hand appliqué.

MACHINE APPLIQUÉ: Trace all of the appliqué patterns, *opposite* and on page 12, onto the paper side of the fusible webbing.

Select a scrap fabric for each shape. Following the manufacturer's directions, fuse the webbing to the wrong sides of the fabrics. Cut out all the shapes, cutting on the traced lines.

HAND APPLIQUÉ: Refer to page 78 for tips on making templates

for appliqué. Make a template for each of the patterns, *opposite* and on page 12. Trace each template onto the appliqué fabric. Cut out each shape, adding a ³/₁₆-inch seam allowance.

Making the appliqué blocks
Center each appliqué on a muslin square, turning the square on point. Appliqué by hand or by machine as described below.

When the appliqué is complete, use a permanent-ink marker to add details, such as the pig's face and the kite tail.

MACHINE APPLIQUÉ: Set your sewing machine to make a tight, narrow zigzag stitch. Experiment with scrap fabrics to find the best setting for your machine; practice making points and curves.

You may find that machine appliqué is easier with a piece of typing paper under the muslin fabric as you stitch. As you sew through all layers, the paper acts as a stabilizer to minimize shifting and stretching. Tear the paper away when stitching is complete.

Center each appliqué on one 4½-inch muslin square; fuse the appliqué in place. Zigzag-stitch the edges of each piece, using a matching thread for each fabric.

HAND APPLIQUÉ: Turn under the edges of the appliqué pieces. Pin or baste each piece in the center of a muslin square. Using small hidden stitches, appliqué each piece in place.

Making the peekaboo doors
Match a 4½-inch lining square with a print fabric square for each door. With right sides together, stitch three sides of the square. Clip corners; turn to right side and press. Make 12 doors.

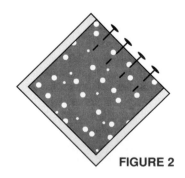

FIGURE 2

Pin the raw edge of each door unit to the upper right edge of an appliquéd muslin square as illustrated in Figure 2, *opposite, below.* The muslin square will be slightly larger on three sides than the stitched door unit.

Completing the blocks

On one appliquéd block, sew a purple triangle onto the raw edge where the door is pinned, sewing through all layers to secure the door. Sew a second purple triangle onto the opposite side of the block, keeping the door out of the way of the seam.

Complete the block with purple triangles on the remaining two sides, keeping the door clear of the stitching.

continued

PEEKABOO CRIB QUILT PATTERNS

11

PEEKABOO CRIB QUILT PATTERNS

Repeat with the remaining triangles of pink, purple, yellow, and blue dotted fabrics to complete all 12 blocks. Press seam allowances toward the triangles.

Sew the border print triangles onto the sides of each block in the same manner. Press the seam allowances toward the print fabric.

Hand-sew matching self-fastening circles onto the appliquéd squares and the door linings.

Assembling the quilt top
Note: Refer to the quilt assembly diagram, *below,* for guidance when assembling the quilt top.

Sew the appliquéd blocks into six diagonal rows with the plain peach blocks and muslin setting triangles positioned as illustrated. Press the seam allowances away from the patchwork blocks.

Stitch the six rows together, matching seam lines where the blocks meet. Add corner triangles to complete the quilt top.

To trim the side triangles, use an acrylic ruler and rotary cutter. Place the ruler's edge ¼ inch beyond the corner of the pieced blocks; cut away the excess fabric on all sides, leaving a ¼-inch seam allowance.

The quilt top now measures approximately 34¼x45½ inches.

Adding the borders
Sew a blue dotted border strip to the top and bottom edges of the quilt top; trim the border fabric even with the sides of the quilt.

Sew two of the remaining border strips together end to end; press the seam allowance to one side. With right sides together,

match the seam line of the border strip to the center of one side of the quilt top; stitch the border in place. Trim excess border fabric at the ends. Sew the border on the opposite side of the quilt in the same manner.

Add the print outer borders in the same manner, sewing top and bottom edges first, then the sides. Press all border seam allowances toward the inner border fabric.

Quilting and finishing
Seam the two panels of backing fabric together; press the seam allowance to one side.

Layer the backing, batting, and quilt top; baste the three layers securely together. Trim the batting and backing fabrics so they are 2 inches larger than the quilt top all around.

Quilt or tie as desired. The quilt pictured on pages 4 and 5 is quilted "in the ditch" (along the seam lines) in the borders and around the triangles of the print border fabrics. The shape of a door and its surrounding triangles are echoed in the quilting in the plain peach squares.

When quilting is complete, trim excess batting and backing even with the quilt top.

Refer to page 79 for tips on how to make and apply binding. From the 2¼-inch-wide strips of the print border fabric, make approximately 230 inches of binding.

Quilted Baby Bib

Shown on page 6.

The finished bib measures approximately 7½x9 inches.

MATERIALS
Two 10-inch squares of white cotton fabric
8x10-inch piece of thin batting, flannel, or fleece
24 inches of ¼-inch-wide ribbon
32 inches of ½-inch-wide flat lace trim
Nonpermanent fabric marker
Tracing paper and pencil
continued

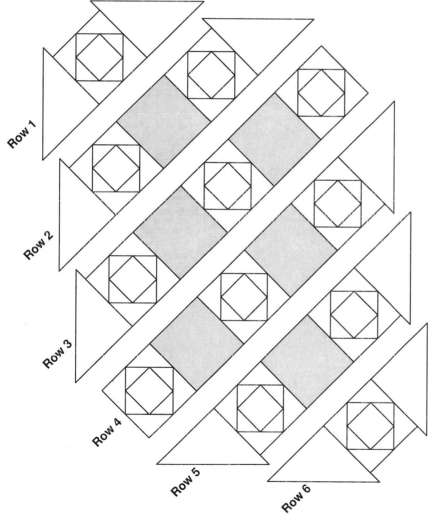

Row 1
Row 2
Row 3
Row 4
Row 5
Row 6

PEEKABOO CRIB QUILT ASSEMBLY DIAGRAM

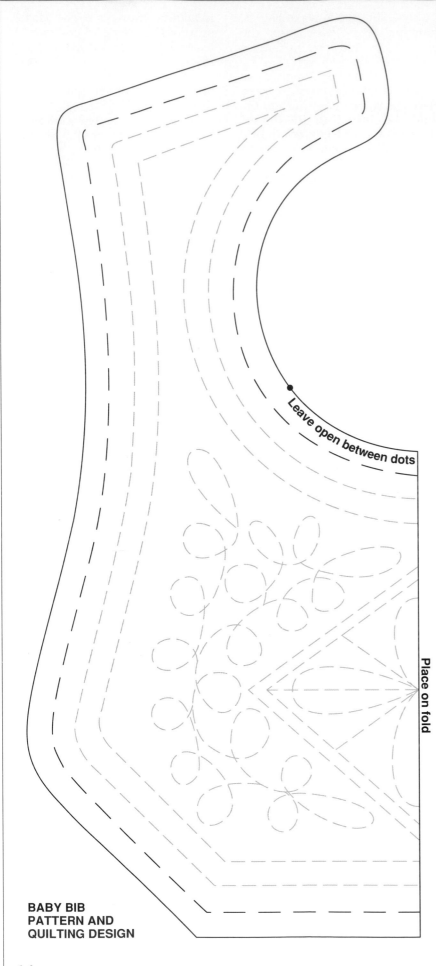

Leave open between dots

Place on fold

**BABY BIB
PATTERN AND
QUILTING DESIGN**

INSTRUCTIONS

The bib pictured on page 6 is quilted by machine, but it also can be quilted by hand. The bib is trimmed with lace, then lined and finished before it is quilted.

Preparing the bib fabric

Trace the bib pattern, *left,* and the quilting design onto paper, making a complete pattern for the bib.

Tape the paper pattern to a windowpane, then tape one white fabric square on top of it. Use a nonpermanent-ink fabric marker to trace all lines and markings onto the fabric.

Cut out the bib shape. Use the paper pattern as a guide to cut a second bib piece from the remaining square of white fabric. Cut one bib shape from the batting.

Assembling the bib

Make a ½-inch hem at both ends of the lace trim to conceal the raw edges. Starting at the back neck of the bib, baste the lace around the outside edge, matching right sides and raw edges. Pleat the lace at the corners to make it lie flat.

Place the two fabric bib pieces with right sides together, then place the batting piece on top. Pin around the edges to prevent the layers from shifting while you stitch.

Machine-stitch around the bib, leaving a small opening at the neck edge for turning, as indicated on the pattern.

Clip the seam allowance at the corners and around the neckline. Turn the bib right side out; hand-sew the opening closed.

Quilting and finishing

Quilt the traced design by hand or by machine. Remove the tracing following the manufacturer's directions that accompany the fabric marker.

Cut the ribbon into two 12-inch lengths. Tack a piece onto the bib on each side of the back neck opening to make ties.

Stenciled Crib Quilt

Shown on page 7.

The finished crib quilt measures approximately 39¾x51¼ inches. Each block is 5¾ inches square.

MATERIALS

2 yards of white fabric
1⅝ yards of backing fabric
45x60-inch piece of batting
Fabric stencil paints in the following colors: rose, blue, purple, magenta, and green
Stencil brushes
Masking tape and art knife
Two 12x18-inch sheets of acetate or stencil plastic
Fabric marker and ruler

INSTRUCTIONS

The quilt shown is a quick and easy stenciling project. These patterns, however, also are very suitable for appliqué. If you prefer to appliqué, substitute ¾ to 1 yard of fabric for each paint color.

Cutting the fabrics

Cut one 25x57-inch piece of the white fabric. Cut this piece into thirty-five 6¼-inch squares.

From the remaining white fabric, cut a 6x42-inch piece for the inside border and an 8x50-inch strip for the outside border. For the stenciled middle border, cut two 4x43-inch strips, two 4x32-inch strips, and four 4-inch squares for the corners.

Preparing stenciling materials

Cut six 5¾-inch squares from the stencil plastic for the block motifs. From the remaining plastic, cut two 3½x5¾-inch pieces for the border motif and two 3½-inch squares for the border corners.

In the patterns *below* and on pages 16 and 17, each number represents one paint color (see color key on page 17). Mark and cut a stencil for each color used on each motif. On each cut stencil, trace the outline of adjacent motifs to serve as guidelines for positioning each stencil atop previously painted areas.

continued

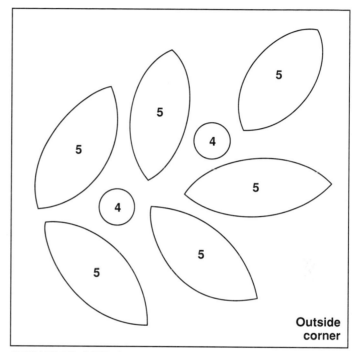

Outside corner

STENCILED CRIB QUILT BORDER CORNER

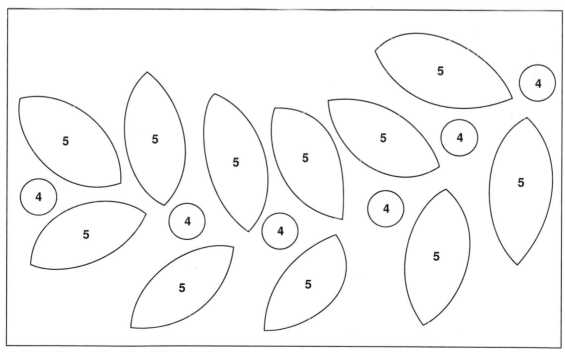

STENCILED CRIB QUILT BORDER MOTIF　　　　**See color key on page 17**

15

STENCILED CRIB QUILT BLOCK A

Stenciling the blocks

Note: Always let the paint on each fabric piece dry completely before adding the next paint color.

Center the stencil for Color 1, Block A, atop one white fabric square. There should be ¼-inch seam allowance on all sides of the stencil. (For more accuracy, draw the seam allowance on the fabric with fabric marker beforehand.)

Tape both the fabric and the stencil to the work surface. Holding the brush upright and using pouncing strokes, stencil the four rose tulips on the fabric. When the paint is dry, add the magenta petals and green leaves.

Stencil 18 of Block A in this manner. Make 17 of Block B, stenciling Color 3 first, then adding colors 2 and 5.

Heat-set the paints according to the manufacturer's directions.

Stenciling the borders

INSIDE BORDER: Cover the entire 6x43-inch piece of white fabric with a solid coat of blue paint. When the paint is completely dry, cut the fabric into four 1½x43-inch strips.

OUTSIDE BORDER: Cut the 8x50-inch fabric into four 2-inch-wide strips. Mark a ¾-inch border on one long side of each strip.

Cover the wider portion of each border strip with a solid coat of rose paint.

STENCILED BORDER: On each of the four border strips, draw a ¼-inch seam line to use as a positioning guide for the stencil.

Draw vertical lines across the strips to mark 5¾-inch segments. Measuring outward from the center of each strip, mark seven segments on the 43-inch borders and five segments on the 32-inch borders. *Note:* Borders are cut slightly longer than needed; do not trim borders until after they are sewn onto the quilt top.

Center the border stencils in each marked segment. Stencil the green leaves, then add magenta berries. Remove markings.

Paint the border corners in the same manner, centering corner stencils on each 4-inch square.

Assembling the quilt

Stitch the stenciled blocks together to make seven horizontal rows of five blocks each. Alternate the A and B blocks in each row. Make

STENCILED CRIB QUILT BLOCK B

four rows that have Block A at each end; make three rows with a Block B at both ends. Join the rows to assemble the quilt top.

Stitch a 43-inch-long blue border strip to both long sides of the quilt. Press the seam allowances toward the border; trim the border fabric even with the ends of the quilt. Sew blue border strips to the top and bottom edges.

Match the center of each 32-inch-long stenciled border with the center of one end of the quilt. Stitch; trim excess border fabric.

Join a corner square onto each end of the remaining long border strips, turning the corner square as necessary to keep the outside corner of the stenciled design (indicated on the pattern on page 15) in its proper position.

Sew the side borders in place, matching the corner seam lines with the end border seams.

Add the outside border in the same manner as the inside border, sewing the rose edge of the fabric onto the quilt top.

Quilting and finishing
Sandwich the batting between the quilt top and the backing fabric; baste all the layers together.

Quilt "in the ditch" on all the seam lines. When quilting is complete, remove basting. Trim batting and backing even with the rose outside border.

Turn under ¼ inch of white fabric around the quilt edge. Turn the remaining edge of white fabric over to the back to make a hem; hand-sew hem in place on the backing.

COLOR KEY
1 = Rose
2 = Purple
3 = Blue
4 = Magenta
5 = Green

Playful Pandas Quilt

Shown on pages 8 and 9.

The finished quilt measures approximately 51 inches square.

MATERIALS

3¾ yards of muslin for bears, checkerboards, and backing
1¼ yards of black fabric
1 yard *each* of red print and cream checked fabrics
¾ yard of yellow print fabric
⅓ yard of green binding fabric
56-inch square of quilt batting
Template material
Black permanent-ink fabric marker
Nonpermanent fabric marker
Rotary cutter, mat, and ruler
1¼ yards of fusible webbing (for machine appliqué only)

INSTRUCTIONS

The quilt shown was appliquéd by machine. Instructions are given for both hand- and machine-appliqué techniques.

Cutting the fabrics

Cut ten 2x42-inch strips of muslin for the checkerboards.

Divide the remaining muslin into two 56-inch lengths. From one panel, cut two 7½x56-inch strips; set these and the large panel aside for the backing.

From the remaining 26x56-inch piece of muslin, cut twelve 8½-inch squares for the appliqué.

Cut eleven 2x42-inch strips of the black fabric for the checkerboards. Save the remaining black fabric for the appliqué.

From the red print fabric, cut four 5-inch squares for corners. For the appliquéd medallion bor-

der, cut two 8x21½-inch strips and two 8x38½-inch strips.

From the yellow fabric, cut four 1½x39-inch strips and twelve 1½x24-inch strips for sashing.

Cut the checked fabric into two 10½-inch squares and two 13¾-inch squares. Cut each square in half diagonally to make four large and four small triangles.

Preparing fabrics for appliqué

Lightly trace the outline of each bear pattern, *below* and *opposite*, onto a muslin square, including all detail and placement lines. *Note:* A water-erasable pen is not recommended because required pressing may set the marks.

Trace four of each bear pattern. Do not cut the muslin yet.

Trace the black parts of each bear onto template material. Cut *continued*

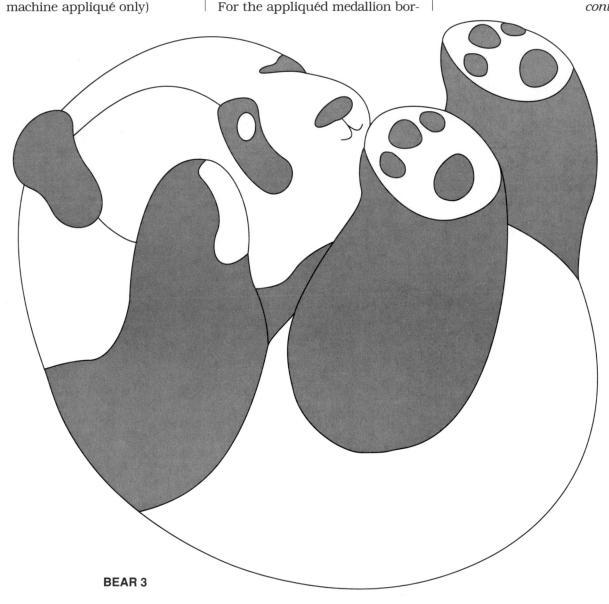

BEAR 3

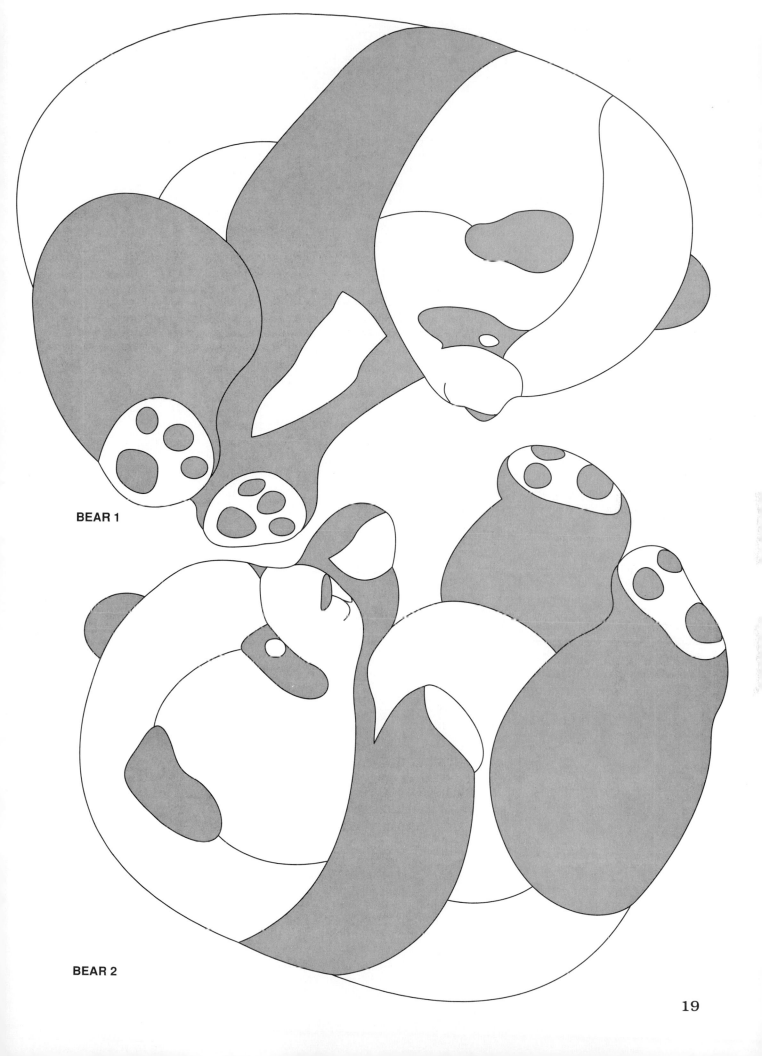

BEAR 1

BEAR 2

19

out the shape on the drawn line to make a template for each part. Mark the number of the bear pattern on each template.

Trace around the templates on the black fabric, using a light-colored fabric marker. Leave ½ inch of space between tracings.

HAND APPLIQUÉ: Cut out each shape from the black and muslin fabrics, adding a 3/16-inch seam allowance around each piece.

MACHINE APPLIQUÉ: Following the manufacturer's instructions, fuse the webbing to the wrong side of the black fabric.

Cut out the black shapes on the traced lines. Fuse each piece in place on a drawn muslin bear. When all the black shapes are fused, cut out the muslin bears.

Appliquéing the pandas
Position one Bear 1 at each end of a 38½-inch-long red strip, approximately 1¾ inches from the fabric edge. Position one Bear 2 and one Bear 3 on the strip, centered between the corner bears. Repeat, positioning four bears on the second 38½-inch-long strip.

Place one each of bears 2 and 3 on each short red strip. Referring to the photo on pages 8 and 9, position each panda 1¼ inches from the center of the strip.

HAND APPLIQUÉ: Turn under the edges of the appliqué pieces. Pin or baste each piece in place on the red fabric as described above. Using small hidden stitches, appliqué each piece.

When appliqué is complete, fill in detail lines, noses, smiles, and paws with black fabric marker.

MACHINE APPLIQUÉ: Fuse all bears onto the red fabric.

Set your sewing machine on a tight, narrow zigzag stitch. Experiment on scrap fabrics to find the best machine setting. Practice stitching points and curves. *Note:* Machine appliqué is sometimes easier if you place a sheet of paper under the bottom fabric; as you sew, the paper keeps the fabric from shifting. Tear the paper away when stitching is complete.

Use black thread to machine-appliqué around each piece.

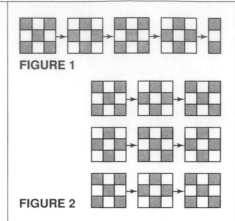

FIGURE 1

FIGURE 2

Making the checkerboards
Use the 2-inch-wide strips of muslin and black fabrics for the checkerboard center and borders.

TRADITIONAL PIECING: Cut the strips into 2-inch squares.

STRIP PIECING: To make Strip Set A, stitch one muslin strip between two black strips. Make four of Strip Set A.

Make Strip Set B in the same manner, *except* change the fabric placement to one black strip between two strips of muslin. Make three of Strip Set B.

Press all the seam allowances toward the black fabric.

Cut each strip set into twenty-one 2-inch-wide units. Cut 70 units from the A strip sets and 61 units from the B strip sets.

BORDERS: For each border, assemble four nine-patch squares as illustrated in Figure 1, *top.* Join these squares in a row as shown, ending the row with one extra A unit.

Make eight border sections.

CENTER: For the center checkerboard, assemble nine nine-patch squares as illustrated in Figure 2, *above.* Join the squares in three horizontal rows as shown, then sew the rows together.

Assembling the center diamond
Stitch two smaller triangles of checked fabric onto opposite sides of the center checkerboard; press seam allowances toward the triangles. Add triangles to the remaining sides of the square.

Stitch a 24-inch-long strip of yellow fabric to opposite sides of the center square; press seam al-

lowances toward the yellow fabric. Trim yellow fabric even with the sides of the square. Sew yellow strips to the remaining sides.

Add the appliquéd red strips in the same manner, matching the center of each strip with the center of each side of the square.

Finish the center diamond by adding the 39-inch-long strips of yellow fabric. Measuring ¼ inch beyond the red corners, trim the ends of the yellow border corners.

Adding the quilt corners
Refer to Figure 3, *below,* as a guide to assemble each corner unit as described here, using the remaining triangles of checked fabric and yellow strips.

Sew a yellow fabric strip onto one short leg of a checked triangle, aligning one end of the strip with the right-angle corner.

Add another yellow strip to the adjacent short leg of the triangle. The yellow strips are longer than necessary; do not trim the excess at this time. Press the seam allowances toward the yellow fabric.

Stitch a checkerboard border strip to one side of the triangle, aligning one end of the border with the triangle corner.

Sew a red corner square onto one end of another checkerboard border; press the seam allowance toward the red fabric. Stitch this pieced border onto the triangle unit, completing the corner unit illustrated in Figure 3, *below.*

Trim the yellow and checkerboard borders to align with the angle of the triangle as shown.

Make three more corner units in the same manner.

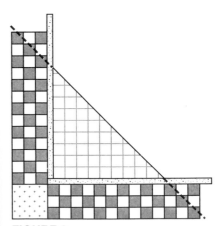

FIGURE 3

Sew a corner triangle unit onto opposite sides of the center diamond. Press the seams toward the quilt center. Repeat to add corners to the remaining sides.

Quilting and finishing
Sew a 7½-inch-wide muslin strip to each side of the large muslin piece to make a 56-inch square of backing fabric. Sandwich the batting between the backing and the quilt top; baste the three layers securely together.

Quilt as desired. The quilt pictured is quilted "in the ditch" along each seam line and through the middle of the center checkerboard. When quilting is complete, remove basting; trim batting and backing even with the quilt top.

Refer to page 79 for tips on how to make and apply binding. Make approximately 5¾ yards of binding, using the green dotted fabric.

Panda Diaper Bag

Shown on page 9.

The finished bag measures approximately 19x22 inches.

MATERIALS
1 yard *each* of cream checked fabric and muslin
½ yard of black fabric
1½x13-inch piece *each* of yellow and red print fabrics
38-inch square of quilt batting
Template material
Black permanent-ink fabric marker
Nonpermanent fabric marker
Rotary cutter, mat, and ruler
¼ yard of fusible webbing (for machine appliqué only)

INSTRUCTIONS

Cutting the fabrics
From *each* of the muslin, checked fabric, and the batting, cut one 24x38-inch rectangle for the bag and one 10½x13-inch piece for the pocket. On the checked fabric only, trim the pocket piece to 9x13 inches.

From the black fabric, cut two 5x42-inch strap pieces and two 2¼x24-inch strips for binding.

Reserve scraps of muslin and black fabric for the appliqué.

Making the pocket
Stitch the strips of yellow and red print fabrics together along one 13-inch side. Join the yellow side of the combined strip to one 13-inch edge of the checked pocket fabric. Press all seam allowances toward the yellow fabric.

Baste batting to muslin pocket piece. With right sides together, sew the muslin to the checked pocket fabric. Stitch around all four sides, leaving a 3-inch opening in the bottom edge.

Clip the corners and trim the seams, then turn the pocket right side out through the opening. Hand-sew the opening closed.

Refer to the instructions for the Playful Pandas Quilt, *opposite,* for detailed appliqué directions. Select any one of the three panda patterns on pages 18 and 19. Appliqué the panda on the pocket, stitching through all layers.

Pin the appliquéd pocket on the checked bag fabric, placing the top (red) edge of the pocket approximately 4 inches from the top edge of the bag and 6½ inches from the side edges.

Topstitch the pocket in place, stitching ⅛ inch from the edge around the pocket sides and bottom. Make a second row of stitching ¼ inch inside the first row.

Assembling the bag
Layer the batting between the muslin lining and the bag fabric. Machine-baste the three layers together, stitching ½ inch from the edge on all sides.

Fold the bag in half with right sides together. Stitch a 1-inch seam at both sides. Press the seam allowances to one side.

There are several ways to enclose the raw edges of these seam allowances. Our bag was made with flat-fell seams. At each seam, trim the underneath seam allowance to ¼ inch. Fold the top seam allowance in half, then smooth it flat over the first seam allowance, enclosing all raw edges. Topstitch the seam allowance in place, sewing close to the edge of the seam allowance.

To finish the corners, flatten the bag with one side seam in the center front so the corner forms a triangle as shown in Figure 1, *below.* Measuring 2 inches from the tip of the triangle, machine-stitch through all layers of the bag.

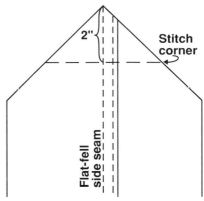

FIGURE 1

Repeat for the other bag corner. You can cut off the triangle points or leave them flat inside the bag. Turn the bag right side out.

Making the bag straps
With right sides facing, fold one 42-inch-long strip of black fabric in half lengthwise; stitch the long edges together. Repeat for the second strip. Turn each strip right side out through the open ends.

Press both strips with the seam line at one edge.

Topstitch along both sides of each strip, ⅛ inch from the edge. Repeat, stitching ¼ inch inside the first stitching line.

Baste one end of each strap to the top inside edge of the bag approximately 5½ inches from the side seams, matching the end of the strap with the raw edge of the muslin. Baste the opposite end of the strap to the opposite edge of the bag. Leave the straps inside the bag while you bind the edges.

Binding the top edge of the bag
Sew the binding strips together end to end; press the seam open.

Refer to page 79 for tips on how to make and apply binding. Following those instructions, stitch binding to the front of the bag. Be sure the strap ends are caught in the stitching. Turn the binding to the wrong side; hand-sew it in place onto the muslin lining.

FUN ON THE FARM

A PLAYTIME BOOK OF MAKE-BELIEVE

With these fanciful projects, you can treat your child to a delightful day in the country every day. Witty animal themes are a perennial favorite of the younger set, and these cute critters will amuse till the cows come home.

Horses frolic and cows cavort in all the games of pretend promised by our fantasy farm, *left* and *below*.

Assembled in a book format, the farm and its endearing hand-size creatures are portable make-believe fun at the sitter's, in the car, or in a quiet corner at home.

A red felt barn is appliquéd on the sky-blue cover. The doors open to reveal felt stalls, each embroidered with the name of the animal tucked inside it.

Rolling hills inside the book form pockets that hold the felt animals in place during imaginary wanderings.

Instructions and patterns for the Play Farm begin on page 24.

Count on sweet dreams when you tuck your child in beneath the whimsical lamb quilt, *left*. White-faced ewes are appliquéd onto grass-green blocks, with a single black sheep, *below*, amidst the flock.

Directions for the quilt begin on page 30.

Play Farm Book

Shown on pages 22 and 23.

Folded book measures 11x12 inches.

MATERIALS
Two 13x23-inch light blue cotton rectangles for book cover
One 13x23-inch piece of batting
Two squares of red felt
4 squares of light green felt
3 squares of tan felt
2 squares each of white, light blue, dark green, and dark brown felt
1 square each of dark gray, light gray, black, and pink felt
Tracing paper; graph paper
Sewing threads to match felt
2-inch strip of self-grip fastening tape
Red, yellow, green, brown, black, tan, and white embroidery floss
Dressmaker's carbon paper
Water-erasable pen; crafts glue
Polyester fiberfill

INSTRUCTIONS
To make the book base
Pin and baste the batting rectangle to the wrong side of one blue rectangle. With right sides of the two blue fabrics facing, and using ½-inch seams, sew through all thicknesses, leaving an opening for turning. Trim batting close to seams; trim blue fabric and clip curves; turn. Sew opening closed.

To trim the cover
Trace the full-size half of the barn top pattern, *opposite*, onto tracing paper; cut out the pattern. Use the graph paper to draw and cut a 1¾x5-inch rectangle pattern for the sides of the barn. Draw and cut a 4x5-inch rectangle pattern for the barn doors. Draw and cut a 1½x1¾-inch rectangle pattern for the loft doors.

On folded red felt, cut 1 barn top. Cut two *each* of the barn sides and both sets of doors from red felt.

Using the carbon paper, trace and transfer the Book Title Pattern on page 26 to the top of the felt barn below the loft area. Use three strands of yellow floss to outline-stitch the title.

Whipstitch the side pieces to the sides of the barn.

Referring to the Barn Diagram on page 26, cut ¼-inch-wide strips of white felt to trim the barn and doors. Hand-sew the strips to the red felt pieces. (The back sides of the barn doors also have white felt trim.)

Tack the sides of the loft doors to the top of the barn. Tack the doors closed or leave them open.

For the stable background, cut a 5½x10¼-inch tan rectangle. For the animal stalls, refer to the Barn Stall Diagram on page 27 to draw patterns onto graph paper as follows. *Note:* The stall patterns overlap one another. For example, the pig stall overlaps the cow stall. The gates on the cow and horse stalls are solid doors. The gates on the pig, goat, and sheep stalls are slats; cut these slats after cutting out the solid gates first.

For the cow stall, draw a 4⅝x4¼-inch rectangle. Using the measurements on the diagram, complete the pattern for this stall. For the horse stall, draw a 5½x4¼-inch rectangle; use the measurements to complete the pattern. For the pig stall, draw a 1¾x2¾-inch rectangle; use the measurements to complete the slatted gate. For the sheep stall, draw a 1½x2¾-inch rectangle; use the measurements to complete the slatted gate. For the goat stall, draw a 3x2¾-inch rectangle; add the slatted gate.

Cut two of each stall from tan felt. Cut ¼-inch-wide strips from tan felt to trim each piece as shown on the pattern diagram. Whipstitch each of the matching stall pieces together, adding the ¼-inch trim pieces along the border edges as you sew. Add the additional trim pieces. Outline-stitch the animal names on each stall with three strands of red embroidery floss.

Hand-sew the background and stall pieces to the blue cover in the following sequence: Center and line up the 10¼-inch edge of the stable background with the

bottom edge of the front (folded book) cover, and sew in place. Line up the cow and horse stalls with the top and side edges on each side of the stable background. Whipstitch these stalls to the tan background along the top, the 4¼-inch sides, and up to the gate only on the bottom edge. Line up the pig and goat stalls with the bottom and sides of the cow and horse stalls; whipstitch the sides and bottom edges up to the gate to the background/stall piece. Line up the sheep stall with the bottom and side edge of the goat stall; whipstitch the side and bottom up to the gate to the background/stall piece.

Center and hand-sew the barn to the blue cover. Do not sew around the door opening. Securely tack the barn doors only at the sides of the barn door openings (do not tack doors to the stalls). Trace and cut latch patterns on page 26, and cut as directed on pattern pieces. Sew the felt piece on top of the large latch. Matching the pieces, sew the large latch to the left door; sew the felt latch to the right door.

To make the landscape
The landscape in our book includes appliquéd "pocket" meadow, bushes, and rocks for the animals to stand behind. These provide part of the fun of playing with this book.

Use the Landscape Diagram on page 27 as a guide to draw your basic landscape on a 12x21½-inch piece of graph or tracing paper in the following order. First draw diagonal stream (1). The triangular area below the stream is meadow (2). Draw meadow (3) along the horizon and extend it to either the stream or 1 inch below and behind meadow (4). Draw rolling hill meadow (4), extending it to the stream. Piece and cut the stream from light blue felt; cut meadows (2) and (3) from light green felt; cut two each of meadow (4) from light green felt and sew the top two edges of meadow (4) together.

Referring to the photo on page 23, embroider assorted colors of French knot flowers with green straight-stitch stems and leaves atop meadows (2) and (4). Embroider clumps of long-stitch greenery along bases of rocks. Add long-stitch cattails among the rocks along the stream.

If desired, draw basic shapes of rabbits, chickens, and ducks (see patterns on page 27) onto the landscape pieces with the water-erasable pen. Fill in these shapes with long and short stitches, split stitches, chain stitches, or satin stitches using embroidery floss colors of your choice.

In the same sequence as you drew and cut them, hand-sew the four basic shapes to the blue background fabric (do not fasten the top edge of meadow [4]). *Note:* If the pieces do not fit exactly, you can cover them with bushes and rocks as you proceed to trim the basic landscape pieces.

Draw four tree trunks onto the paper landscape. Draw cloudlike shapes for the foliage. Trace and cut the trunks from dark brown felt; cut the foliage from dark green felt. Hand-sew the trees to the landscape.

Draw shrubs, rocks, and banks onto your paper drawing to add dimension along the stream and additional shrubs and rocks to make the landscape interesting. Trace and cut two matching felt pieces of each of these shapes for durability and pockets. Cut rocks from dark and light gray felt; cut shrubs from dark green felt; cut banks from tan felt.

Arrange the felt pieces on your fabric landscape. Decide what bushes, rocks, or bank pieces will be pockets, and whipstitch the top edges of those matching pieces together. Sew all these pieces in place, leaving pocket edges free.

Cut six dark brown 1½x¼-inch felt posts, and sew along the top edge of meadow (3.) With one strand of dark brown embroidery floss, couch a barbed wire fence.

For the animals
HORSE: Trace and cut two body patterns on page 28 from light brown felt. With both pieces together, and beginning at the front legs and stitching toward the back legs, sew legs together, stuffing each leg with fiberfill as you sew. Stitch up to tail position. For the tail, cut nine 4-inch-long strands of brown floss. Knot the strands together at one end. In-

sert the knot between the felt pieces and continue to join the felt pieces together to the base of the mane. Stuff the body. For the mane, cut 4-inch-long strands of brown floss. Lay ¼-inch ends of strands between felt pieces. With backstitches, join the felt pieces together along the mane area, securing the floss strands at the same time. Join head and neck areas, stuffing as you go. Sew remaining body together and stuff as required. Trim mane and tail.

continued

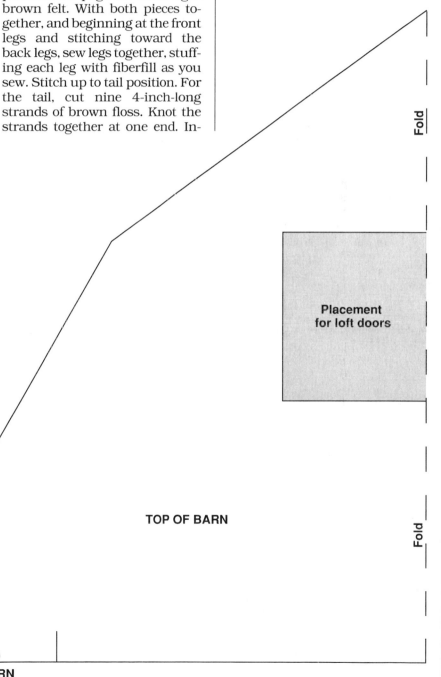

Fold

Placement
for loft doors

Fold

TOP OF BARN

Barn side

½ OF BARN PATTERN

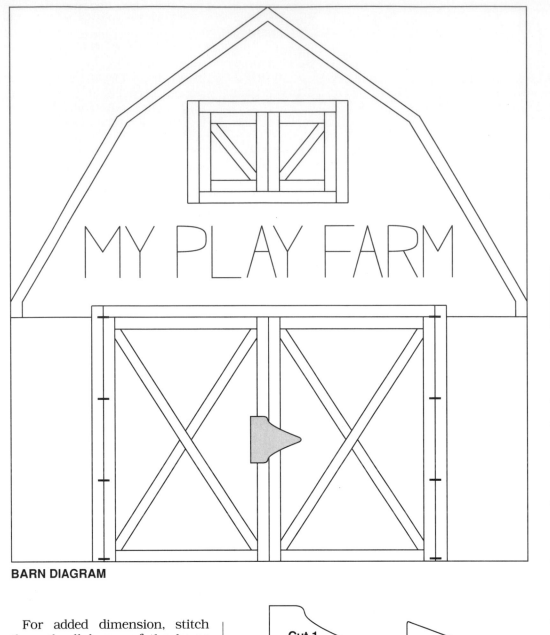

BARN DIAGRAM

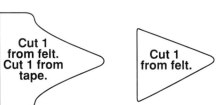

Cut 1 from felt. Cut 1 from tape.

Cut 1 from felt.

BARN DOOR LATCH PATTERNS

BOOK TITLE PATTERN

For added dimension, stitch through all layers of the horse with matching thread, following the blue lines on the pattern. Use black floss to embroider eyes, nose, mouth, and hooves. Cut a white felt diamond and sew to forehead.

COLT: Follow the instructions for the horse, except cut six strands of floss, each 3 inches long, for the tail. Trim the mane to ¼ inch. Cut two of each spot from white felt and sew spots to each side of body. Add dimensional stitching; embroider eyes, nose, mouth, and hooves.

COW: Using the pattern on page 28, trace and cut two black felt body pieces. Cut two of each spot

from white felt and sew spots to each body side. Cut one white blaze and sew to front of head. Cut two pink felt udders and sew to each side of body. For the tail, tie one 4-inch-long piece of 6-strand white floss around the center of a 6-inch-long strand of black floss. Pick the white strands apart with the tip of a straight pin to make them bushy; trim the tail. Fold the black floss
continued

26

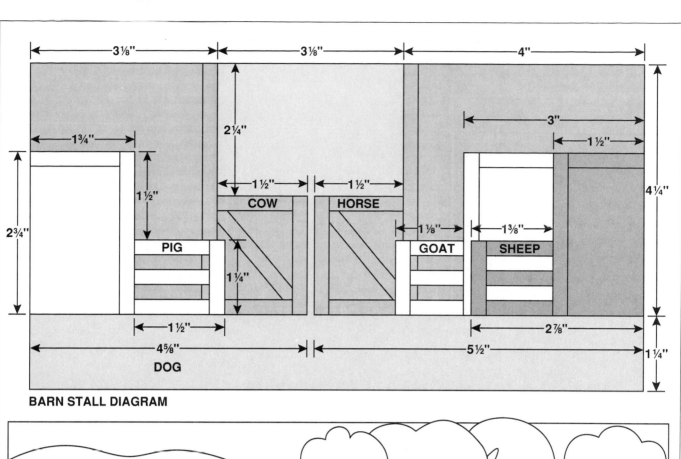

BARN STALL DIAGRAM

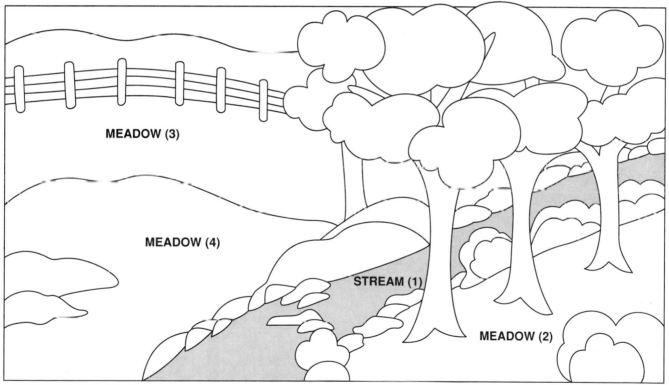

LANDSCAPE DIAGRAM

EMBROIDERED ANIMALS FOR LANDSCAPE

HORSE

COLT

COW

CALF

FARM ANIMAL PATTERNS

in half, and twist the lengths together. Run glue along the length of the black strands to hold the strands together. Sew the body together in the same manner as the horse, stuffing as you go. Sew atop the dotted lines to add dimension. With white floss, satin-stitch horns; with brown floss satin-stitch eyes and nose. Use running stitches or split stitches to fill in feet and hooves.

CALF: Follow the instructions for the cow, except make the body from white felt, the spots from black felt, and reverse the floss colors for the tail.

PIG: Trace the body pattern, *top right,* and cut two body pieces from gray felt. For the tail, coat a 6-inch length of gray floss (all six strands) with glue, and shape it into a curl around a pencil; let dry. Sew bodies together, stuffing as you sew and inserting tail as you join the pieces. Follow the blue lines on the pattern to add the dimensional stitching. Embroider mouth, eyes, and nose with black floss.

GOAT: Trace the body pattern, *right,* and cut two body pieces from tan felt. Sew body pieces together, stuffing as you sew. Add the dimensional stitching. Use the brown floss to embroider eyes, nose, mouth, and hooves.

SHEEP: Trace the body pattern, *right,* and cut two body pieces from white felt. Assemble as for Goat. Add the dimensional stitching. Embroider white French knots over both sides of body to form wool. Fill in ears with long stitches, using white floss. Use black floss to embroider eyes, nose, mouth, and hooves.

DOG: Trace the body pattern, *far right,* and cut two body pieces from tan felt; cut spots from white felt. Assemble as for other animals and add the dimensional stitching. Use dark brown to embroider eyes and nose. Add turkey-work embroidery for the tuft at the top of the head, using tan embroidery floss.

FARM ANIMAL PATTERNS

29

Little Lamb Quilt

Shown on pages 22 and 23.

The finished quilt measures approximately 58x88 inches. Each block is 15 inches square.

MATERIALS
5⅜ yards of dark emerald green fabric for blocks and backing
1⅜ yards *each* of medium green and light green fabrics
1¼ yards of green and white striped fabric for the border
Fourteen 9x12-inch scraps of black-on-white print fabrics for the lamb bodies
One 9x12-inch scrap of black print fabric for the black lamb
½ yard *each* of solid cream and black fabrics for lamb faces and legs and the quilt binding
¼ yard of red fabric for corners
72x90-inch precut quilt batting
13½ yards of ¼-inch-diameter white cord or string
Template material
Black and pink embroidery floss
2 yards of fusible webbing (for machine appliqué only)

INSTRUCTIONS
Cutting the fabrics
Cut the dark green fabric into two 96-inch lengths. From one panel, cut two 13x96-inch pieces. Set these and the remaining large panel aside for the backing.

From the remaining dark green fabric and *each* of the medium and light green fabrics, cut five 15½-inch squares to make a total of 15 blocks.

For the picket fence border, cut seven 7x42-inch strips across the width of the striped fabric. Cut four 7-inch squares of red fabric for the border corners.

Cut a 3x12-inch piece from one corner of the black fabric; set aside the remaining black fabric for the binding.

Preparing fabrics for appliqué
Following the red lines on the pattern, *opposite,* trace the lamb body onto template material, joining the two halves of the pattern. Cut the template on the traced line, including the area under the ear as indicated by the dotted line on the pattern.

Following the blue lines, make a template for the face/ear piece, including the area under the head as indicated. Make a template for each leg.

HAND APPLIQUÉ: Trace each template shape (body, head, and legs) directly onto the right side of the appropriate appliqué fabric. Trace six lambs that face to the right, then turn the templates over to trace nine lambs (including the black one) that will face to the left. Cut out each shape, adding a ³/₁₆-inch seam allowance.

MACHINE APPLIQUÉ: Following the manufacturer's instructions, fuse the webbing to the wrong side of each appliqué fabric.

Place the body template faceup on the wrong side of one lamb print fabric; trace the shape onto the fusible webbing. Cut out the lamb on the drawn line.

Cut six more black/white lamb bodies and the black sheep body in this manner. Then cut faces and legs for these eight sheep.

Turn the templates over to cut six bodies, faces, and legs that will face in the opposite direction.

Making the appliqué blocks
Center each appliqué on a green square. Use two squares of each green fabric for the six right-facing lambs. Appliqué by hand or by machine as described below.

When the appliqué is finished, embroider the facial details using four strands of pink floss for the black lamb and black floss for the others. Satin-stitch the nose and eye; outline-stitch the lashes.

HAND APPLIQUÉ: Turn under the edges of the appliqué pieces. Pin or baste each piece in place on a green square. Using small hidden stitches, appliqué each piece.

MACHINE APPLIQUÉ: Set your sewing machine to make a tight, narrow zigzag stitch. Experiment with scrap fabrics to find the best setting for your machine; practice making points and curves.

Machine appliqué is sometimes easier with a piece of paper under the bottom fabric as you stitch. As you sew through all layers, the paper acts as a stabilizer that minimizes shifting and stretching. Tear the paper away when stitching is complete.

Center the appliqué on a green square; fuse the fabric in place. Machine-stitch around the edges of each piece, using a matching thread for each fabric.

Assembling the quilt
Sort the blocks in five rows of three blocks each. Each block in the row is a different green fabric, and the sheep in each row face in the same direction.

Lay out the rows on the floor, alternating the directions of the lambs in adjacent rows. Arrange the blocks in each row so that the same green fabrics will be in diagonal lines across the quilt. (Refer to the photo on page 22.)

Stitch the blocks together in rows, then sew the rows together.

Adding the border
Piece the border strips to achieve two strips that are 7x46 inches and two strips that are 7x76 inches. To hide the seam, position the fabrics so that the seam is on the line between a green and a white stripe.

Pin a length of cord 1¾ inches from the long edge of one border strip. Set the sewing machine to its longest stitch length and widest zigzag to machine-couch the cord onto the fabric. (Couching can be done by hand, if you prefer.) Couch a second length of cord 1¾ inches from the opposite edge of the strip. Couch two lines of cord to each border strip.

Sew the longer borders onto the sides of the quilt top; trim excess border fabric.

Stitch red corner squares onto short border strips; sew borders onto top and bottom of quilt top, matching corner seam lines with side borders.

Quilting and finishing
Sew a 13-inch-wide piece of backing fabric to both sides of the large panel. Press seam allowances to one side.

Layer quilt top, batting, and backing fabric; baste. Quilt "in the ditch" of all the seam lines.

Refer to page 79 for tips on how to make and apply binding. Make 300 inches of binding.

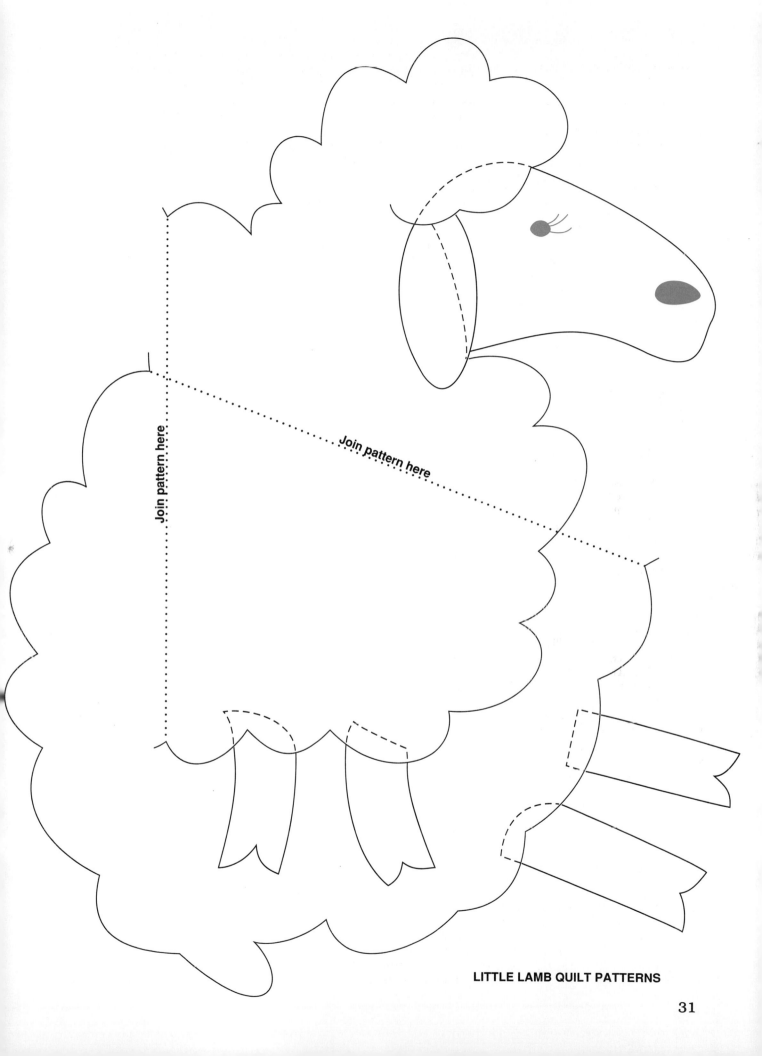

Join pattern here

Join pattern here

LITTLE LAMB QUILT PATTERNS

THE WONDER YEARS

FANTASY QUILTS FOR YOUNG EXPLORERS

Whether your children's flights of fancy find them saddling up or sailing away, blasting off to the moon, or scoring the winning touchdown, capture those fantasies in colorful, just-for-fun quilts. The patchwork and appliquéd projects in this chapter rate high in kid appeal, because they're stitched in the themes that dreams are made of.

Aspiring buckaroos will love your version of this heartwarming cowboy comforter, *left,* a 1930s scrap quilt. It can be made easily with our patterns for the folksy appliquéd wranglers and ponies.

On this treasured old quilt, the cowpokes are cut from lively patterned fabrics typical of '30s textiles, but the design works beautifully with any prints or palette. The ponies are cut from an array of brown and tan fabrics. The hand-embroidered details—the cowboys' lariats, boots, and spurs and tousled ponies' manes—add personality.

The figures are appliquéd onto 9-inch squares, then the quilt top is assembled in diagonal rows of alternating cowboy and pony blocks. The finished size is 73x87 inches.

Just round up some Wild West accessories to coax your child's room into a home-on-the-range mood.

Instructions and patterns are on pages 38 and 39.

With a breezy nautical theme and high-spirited primary colors, these maritime projects will appeal to children of all ages.

Toss our perky Sailor Pillows, *above,* anywhere for a soft, yet lively, accent. Or, borrow the seafaring motifs to embellish a raft of accessories, from quilts to sweatshirts.

These fabric seascapes, featuring rainbow stripes in the lighthouse, boat sail, and all-around piping, are machine-appliquéd, but also may be hand-stitched. Each pillow is 13 inches square. Instructions begin on page 40.

A veritable patchwork regatta cruises over the cheery Sailboat Crib Quilt, *opposite,* a charmer in the nursery. But, since its theme is anything but babyish, on-the-grow kids will love it, too.

Our machine-stitching technique makes launching this project quick and easy. The large sailboat blocks are 8 inches square. The small ones that edge the center medallion are 4 inches square. The finished size of this quilt is approximately 50x60 inches.

Instructions begin on page 42.

For the youngster who daydreams about the space shuttle or the Super Bowl, these notable quilts are stitched with the right stuff.

Our Rocket Power Quilt, *opposite,* harnesses a colorful blast of plaids and prints in an easy-to-piece quilt for the wall or bed. The finished size is approximately 58x72 inches. Stitch more blocks to make a larger quilt.

Instructions begin on page 48.

Young sports fans will cheer the clever football quilt, *above,* a bed-topper and playtime gridiron for scrimmaging with toy figures. Fabrics simulate stadium seating around the playing field. Personalize the quilt with end zone appliqués of your child's name.

The quilt measures 57x76 inches. Directions begin on page 45.

Cowboy Quilt

Shown on pages 32 and 33.

The finished quilt measures approximately 73x87 inches. Each block is 9 inches square.

MATERIALS
6 yards of white fabric
42 assorted 8x11-inch fabric scraps in solid brown, tan, and rust for the horses
30 assorted 7x8-inch print fabric scraps for cowboys
¾ yard of binding fabric
5½ yards of backing fabric
81x96-inch quilt batting
Embroidery floss in yellow, black, brown, and gray
Template material
Nonpermanent fabric marker

INSTRUCTIONS
Instructions are given for hand appliqué. Each horse and cowboy is appliquéd on a plain fabric block, which is set on the diagonal. The quilt is assembled in rows of alternating blocks.

Cutting the fabrics
Make templates for the cowboy and horse patterns, *opposite*. On the appropriate fabrics, trace and cut 42 horses and 30 cowboys, adding a ³/₁₆-inch seam allowance around each piece.

Cut one 28x42-inch piece of white fabric; from this piece, cut six 14-inch squares. Cut each square in quarters *diagonally* to obtain 24 side triangles (this includes two extra).

Cut two 7½-inch squares of white fabric; cut each square in half *diagonally* to get four triangles for the quilt corners.

For the background squares, cut seventy-two 9½-inch squares from the remaining white fabric.

Appliquéing the blocks
Center each white square over one pattern, turning the square on point. Using nonpermanent marker, lightly trace 30 cowboys and 42 horses onto the squares. Include the embroidery details shown in blue on each pattern.

Turn under the seam allowance on each appliqué. Press or baste the seam allowances flat.

Pin each appliqué onto a white square, aligning it with the tracing. Sew the appliqués in place, using a tiny, hidden slip stitch.

Complete the embroidery before joining the blocks. On the quilt pictured, all the cowboys have the same embroidery details—a yellow lariat, black boots, and gray spurs. Use two strands of floss to outline-stitch the boots and lariats. Fill in the boots with satin stitches. Use straight stitches to make the spurs.

Satin-stitch the horses' eyes in black. Use brown floss to outline-stitch the manes.

Assembling the quilt
Refer to the quilt assembly diagram, *below,* to arrange the appliquéd blocks in *diagonal* rows. The horse and cowboy blocks alternate, with a horse block in the first and last positions of each row. Stitch the blocks together with a setting triangle at both ends of each row.

Press seam allowances in one direction in each row, alternating directions of adjacent rows.

Starting at one corner, join the rows. Complete the quilt top by adding the corner triangles.

Finishing and quilting
Divide the backing fabric into two 2¾-yard lengths. Seam the two pieces together; press the seam allowance to one side.

Layer the batting, backing, and quilt top; baste the three layers together. Quilt as desired. The quilt shown on pages 32 and 33 has simple diagonal lines of quilting, spaced 1 inch apart.

When quilting is complete, remove basting; trim batting and backing even with the quilt top.

Cut approximately 330 inches of 2-inch-wide binding. Refer to page 79 for tips on binding.

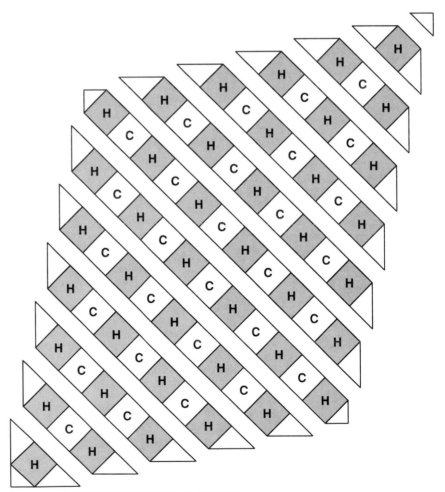

COWBOY QUILT ASSEMBLY DIAGRAM

COWBOY QUILT PATTERNS
Add ³⁄₁₆-inch seam allowance

LIGHTHOUSE PILLOW PATTERN

Sailor Pillows

Shown on page 34.

Each finished pillow measures 13 inches square.

MATERIALS
For two pillows
Two 13½x10½-inch pieces of light blue fabric for skies
Two 3½x13½-inch pieces of ocean-blue fabric
⅝ yard of rainbow-stripe fabric for the sail and the lighthouse
Scraps of red, green, and white fabrics
Four 7½x13½-inch fabric pieces for the pillow backs
Two 13½-inch squares of muslin for appliqué backing
½ yard of paper-backed fusible webbing for machine appliqué
Two 13½-inch squares of quilt batting
Two 10-inch zippers
3 yards of narrow cording
Polyester fiberfill

INSTRUCTIONS
The pillows shown on page 34 are machine-appliquéd. To make these designs by hand, be sure to add seam allowances when cutting the shapes out of the fabric.

For hand appliqué, the fusible webbing is not necessary. Trace each shape directly onto fabric.

Preparing the appliqué fabrics
Trace the patterns, *left* and *opposite,* onto the paper side of the fusible webbing. Make a separate tracing for each piece of the appliqué design.

LIGHTHOUSE PILLOW BLOCK

For the lighthouse and sails, iron the traced fusible webbing onto the wrong side of the striped fabric, following the manufacturer's directions. Position the tracings so that the fabric stripes are horizontal across the patterns.

Following the traced line on the paper, cut out the shape. Cut a boat from the red fabric in the same manner.

Using the block drawings, *opposite bottom* and *far right,* as guides, draw three or more birds and cloud shapes on the webbing. Fuse the webbing onto scraps of white fabric; cut out each shape.

Make two or three shoreline pieces in the same manner; cut these shapes out of green fabric.

Sew the sky and ocean fabrics together to make two 13½-inch squares, one for each pillow.

On the sailboat pillow, center the red boat fabric on the waterline; position sails, birds, and the green shore.

On the lighthouse pillow, position the lighthouse on the right side of the pillow top, then arrange the clouds and shoreline.

Fuse each appliqué piece onto the pillow top. Layer the prepared top, batting, and muslin; baste the layers together.

Appliquéing the designs

Set the sewing machine to make a narrow zigzag stitch. If you are not experienced in machine appliqué, practice on scraps before stitching the pillows. Practice stitching curves and points and pivoting at corners.

Using matching thread colors, machine-appliqué around each shape, sewing through all layers.
continued

SAILBOAT PILLOW BLOCK

**SAILBOAT
PILLOW PATTERN**

Finishing the pillows

Join two backing pieces to make each pillow back, inserting a zipper in the seam. Trim backing to a 13½-inch square.

From the striped fabric, make 53 inches of 1-inch-wide continuous bias for the piping (see tips on bias on page 79). Use a zipper foot to sew the fabric over the cording.

Trim the exposed seam allowance of the piping to ½ inch. Matching raw edges of piping and pillow top, baste piping around the outside edge of the pillow top.

With right sides facing, sew the back onto the pillow top on the ½-inch seam line.

Trim seam allowance and clip corners; turn the pillow right side out through the zipper opening. Be sure to push the corners out completely. Insert stuffing.

Sailboat Crib Quilt

Shown on page 35.

The finished crib quilt measures 50x60 inches. The large sailboat blocks are 8 inches square; the small blocks are 4 inches square.

MATERIALS
1¼ yards of blue solid fabric
¾ yard *each* of blue print, ecru solid, and red solid fabrics
1¾ yards of red checked fabric for borders, medallion sashing, and binding
3¾ yards of backing fabric
1⅞ yards of 48-inch-wide quilt batting
Acrylic ruler
Rotary cutter and mat

INSTRUCTIONS
This quilt features two sizes of sailboat blocks. Fourteen 8-inch blocks sail around the perimeter of the quilt and are framed with sashing. A fifteenth 8-inch block is in the center medallion, framed by two rows of smaller 4-inch sailboat blocks.

Note: Instructions are given for quick-pieced triangles. The fabric cut for quick piecing is large enough to cut individual triangles for traditional piecing, if desired.

Cutting the fabrics
Refer to the block drawing, *below,* for guidance in cutting the fabrics correctly.

From the blue solid fabric, cut four 14-inch squares for the large blocks' triangle-squares, then cut two 7x9-inch pieces and one 5x9-inch piece for the small blocks' triangle-squares.

For the large blocks, cut 15 *each* of these solid blue pieces: 2½x6½ inches (A), 2½x4½ inches (B), and 2½-inch squares (C).

From the remaining blue fabric, cut eight *each* of the following pieces for the small blocks: 1½x3½ inches (A), 1½x2½ inches (B), and 1½-inch squares (C).

Cut and set aside two 2½x37-inch strips of solid red fabric for the sashing squares.

Cut two 14-inch squares from the remaining red fabric. Set one aside for the large blocks' quick-pieced triangles; cut the second square into fifteen 2½x4½-inch D pieces for the large blocks. For the small blocks, cut one 5x9-inch red piece for the triangles and eight 1½x2½-inch D pieces from the remaining red fabric.

From the ecru fabric, cut three 14-inch squares across the width of the fabric; cut two 7x9-inch pieces. Cut four 4½-inch ecru squares for border corners.

For the center medallion, cut two 9-inch squares and a 2½x24-inch strip from the ecru fabric. Cut both squares in half diagonally to make four triangles.

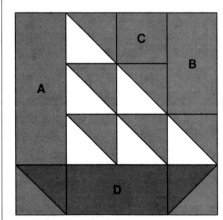

SAILBOAT BLOCK

From the blue print fabric, cut three 8½x37-inch strips for the sashing and two 1½x24-inch strips for the medallion.

For the red checked borders, cut two 4½x54-inch strips and two 4½x44-inch strips. Cut four red checked 1½x17-inch strips and two 1½x29-inch strips for the medallion sashing.

Making the triangle-squares
Each sailboat block has eight triangle-squares—six are blue/ecru and two are blue/red (see the block diagram, *below left*).

Note: Refer to the tips on quick-pieced triangle-squares, *opposite,* for more complete instructions. For traditional piecing, mark the fabrics as instructed and as illustrated in Figure 1, *below,* and Figure 2, on page 44. Then cut the individual triangles apart before you do any stitching.

● Mark a 4x4-square grid of 2⅞-inch squares on the wrong side of one 14-inch ecru fabric square. (See Figure 1, *below.*)

● Place the ecru fabric right sides together with a matching blue square, with the marked side on top. Pin the layers together.

Stitch ¼ inch from both sides of each *diagonal* line (indicated by the red lines in Figure 1).

● Cut the stitched grid apart on all the *drawn* lines, cutting 32 triangle-squares.

● For the large blocks, complete three blue/cream grids and one grid of blue/red. Discarding the extras of each combination, press 90 blue/ecru triangle-squares and 30 blue/red triangle-squares.

continued on page 44

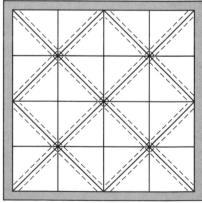

FIGURE 1

Making Quick-Pieced Triangle-Squares

The triangles for triangle-squares can be cut and pieced individually, if you prefer, but this fast and easy machine-stitched method definitely will save you time.

Sewing the triangle-squares on a large piece of fabric eliminates the tedious task of marking triangles with a template, cutting each one out, and sewing them together one by one. With this technique, a few minutes of sewing results in a pile of ready-to-go, accurately sized triangle-squares.

This method is most useful for making many triangle-squares from the same combination of two fabrics. If you want a quilt with more of a "scrappy" look, use this method with small grids of several different fabric combinations, or use scrap-bag fabrics and make the triangle-squares in the traditional way.

Fabric requirements

In this book, the size of the fabric needed for the quick-piecing grid is stated in the project instructions. This size allows a margin of at least 1 inch all around the outside of the grid.

Marking the grid

The only tools needed are a ruler and a marker. Use a pencil, a washable marker, or a permanent-ink marker. Do not use an ordinary ballpoint pen because the ink may run when the finished quilt is washed.

It is best to work with fabric pieces that are no larger than 18x22 inches.

The project instructions always include a description and an illustration of the required quick-piecing grid. Because each square is sewn and cut into *two* finished triangle-squares, the drawn grid squares equal half the number of triangle-squares needed to make the quilt.

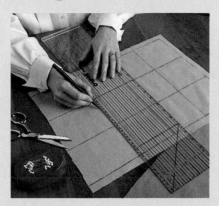

1 Mark a grid of squares on the *wrong side* of the light fabric. The size of each square, which is stated in the project instructions, must be ⅞ inch *larger* than the desired *finished* size of the triangle-square. For example, if you want a 2-inch finished triangle-square, each grid square is 2⅞ inches square. Fill in horizontal and vertical lines to complete the grid as shown *above*.

3 Machine-stitch ¼ inch from *both* sides of all the *diagonal* lines. Pivot the fabric at corners without lifting the needle.

Press the stitched piece. Trim excess fabric around the outside of the grid.

2 Draw a diagonal line through each square, with lines going in the opposite direction in adjacent squares as pictured *above*. Put the marked fabric right sides together on the darker fabric, with the marked fabric on top; press, then pin the layers together. Pin along the horizontal and vertical lines, away from intersections of diagonal lines, so the pins are not in your way as you sew.

4 Cut the fabric into squares by cutting on all the horizontal and vertical grid lines. Next cut on the diagonal lines between the rows of stitching, cutting each square into two triangle-squares.

Open the triangle-squares and press the seam allowances toward the darker fabric. Cut off the "points" of the seam allowances before you proceed. As you handle the triangle-squares, be careful not to pull on the seam lines, as this will stretch the bias and result in a distorted square.

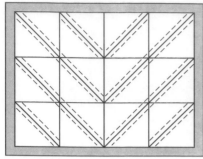

FIGURE 2

● For the small blocks, refer to Figure 2, *above;* mark a 3x4-square grid of 1⅞-inch squares on each 7x9-inch piece of ecru fabric. Stitch both of these grids; cut and press 48 blue/ecru triangle-squares.

In the same manner, mark a 2x4 grid of 1⅞-inch squares on the 5x9-inch red fabric pieces. Sew and cut 16 red/blue triangle-squares.

Assembling the sailboat blocks
Refer to the block assembly diagram, *below,* to piece the sailboat blocks. Beginning with the small blocks, join the triangle-squares and the blue A and B pieces in vertical rows as shown. Join these rows. Assemble and add the red/blue "boat" strip at the bottom as illustrated.

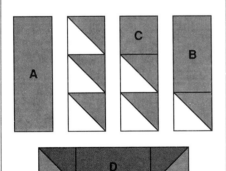

SAILBOAT BLOCK ASSEMBLY DIAGRAM

Make four small sailboat blocks as shown in the block diagram and four blocks that "sail" in the opposite direction.

Stitch 15 large sailboat blocks in the same manner—make seven blocks that "sail" one way and eight mirror-image blocks.

SAILBOAT QUILT ASSEMBLY DIAGRAM

Making the center medallion
Referring to the quilt assembly diagram, *above,* to position the blocks correctly, join four small sailboat blocks in a row; make two rows. Sew a 1½x17-inch red checked sashing strip to top and bottom edges of each row.

Sew a 1½x24-inch blue print strip to both sides of the 24-inch-long ecru strip.

Bring the upper left corner of the strip down to the bottom edge so that the folded fabric forms a right-angle triangle. Crease the fold, then open the fabric flat again. Mark the diagonal made by

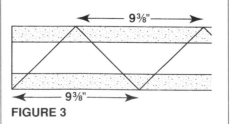

FIGURE 3

the crease from the bottom edge of the strip to the top edge.

Referring to Figure 3, *below left,* measure 9⅜ inches along the bottom edge of the strip; draw a connecting line from the top of the first line to the bottom edge. Continue marking the strip as shown in Figure 3. Cut four triangles apart on the drawn lines.

Sew one striped triangle onto two opposite sides of one large sailboat block. Press seam allowances toward sailboat. Sew the remaining two triangles onto the remaining block sides; press.

Stitch the ecru triangles to the medallion square in the same manner as the striped triangles.

Sew one row of small sailboats to the top and bottom edges of the medallion block. Finish the medallion by adding long strips of red checked fabric on both sides.

Making the pieced sashing

Seam a red sashing strip to both sides of one blue print sashing strip; press the seam allowances toward the blue fabric. Cut fourteen 2½-inch-wide vertical segments from the pieced strip.

Cut 28 more sashing pieces, each 2½x8½ inches, from the remaining blue print strips.

Assembling the quilt top

Refer to the quilt assembly diagram, *opposite,* for guidance while assembling the quilt top.

To make the top row, sew a plain sashing strip to both top and bottom edges of four blocks; press seams toward sashing. Sew a sashing-square strip to the *left* side of each block; join the four blocks in a row. Sew a sashing-square strip to the right side of the last block. Make the bottom row in the same manner.

Stitch a plain sashing strip to both *sides* of each remaining sailboat block. Join these blocks into two vertical rows, sewing a sashing-square strip between blocks.

Sew a vertical row to each side of the center unit. Join top and bottom rows to middle section.

Adding the borders

Sew the longer border strips to the quilt sides; trim excess fabric.

Sew an ecru corner square to one end of both remaining border strips. Measure the length of each strip against the width of the quilt top; trim excess border fabric. Sew the two remaining corner squares onto the trimmed border strips. Sew borders to top and bottom of quilt, matching the seam line of the corner squares with the side border seams.

Quilting and finishing

Cut the backing fabric into two 1⅞-yard lengths. Seam the two panels together; press seam allowance to one side.

Layer the backing, batting, and quilt top; baste. Quilt as desired. When quilting is complete, trim excess batting and backing.

Cut 6½ yards of 2½-inch-wide binding from the red checked fabric. Refer to the tips on page 79 for making and applying binding.

Football Quilt

Shown on page 37.

The finished quilt measures approximately 51x76 inches.

MATERIALS
2 yards of red print fabric for stadium and binding
1½ yards of green print fabric
¾ yard of blue print fabric
½ yard *each* of tan and gray print fabrics
¼ yard *each* of red and white solid fabrics
6x8-inch scrap of brown fabric
3½ yards of backing fabric
60x80 inches of low-loft batting
8 yards of ¼-inch-wide white satin ribbon
2 yards of ½-inch-wide red satin ribbon
½ yard of paper-backed fusible webbing
White fabric marker
White fabric paint and stencil brush
Purchased 1-inch number stencils for yard-line markers
Purchased alphabet stencils for end-zone letters (optional)
Rotary cutter, mat, and ruler

INSTRUCTIONS

These instructions are given for machine stitching, including the use of a machine satin stitch for the appliqué and some details. If you wish to sew by hand, use additional white ribbon to make the yard-line markers.

Cutting the fabrics

Set aside ½ yard of red print fabric for binding. Cut the remainder into two 12½x42-inch strips; cut the strips into six 11½x12½-inch pieces for the stadium sections.

For the playing field, cut one 22½x40½-inch piece of the green fabric. From the remaining green fabric, cut two 6½x22½-inch end zones and four 9½x14½-inch pieces for the stadium corners.

From the blue fabric, cut a strip 12½x42 inches; cut this into four 10x12½-inch pieces for the stadium side sections. Cut two 9½x20½-inch blue pieces for the end-zone sections.

Cut six 3x42-inch strips of tan fabric for the sidelines.

Cut four 2x42-inch strips of gray fabric. Cut these strips into eight 2x12½-inch pieces for the aisles separating the side sections and four 2x9½-inch pieces for the end-zone aisles.

Cut seven 22½-inch lengths of white ribbon for the 20- and 50-yard lines and end zones; cut two 57½-inch lengths for sidelines. Cut three 22½-inch red ribbons for the 20- and 50-yard lines.

Stitching the playing field

Using the white marker and a ruler, mark a parallel line 2¼ inches from the 22½-inch edge of the large green field piece.

Mark 18 parallel lines 2 inches apart down the field. The last line should also be 2¼ inches from the fabric edge. These are the sewing lines for the yard lines.

For the 20- and 50-yard lines, center a piece of white ribbon over each red ribbon piece; pin each ribbon in place on the lines. Topstitch on both sides of the white ribbon.

Adjust the sewing machine to make a wide, tight satin stitch. With white thread, stitch the 10-, 30-, and 40-yard lines.

Note: It may help to place a piece of paper under each line before sewing the satin stitch. The paper stabilizes the fabric and facilitates smoother stitching.

The 5-, 15-, 25-, 35-, and 45-yard lines are stitched with machine quilting later.

Appliquéing the football

Place the fusible webbing over the half-football pattern on page 47 with the paper side up; trace the shape onto the webbing. Turn the webbing upside down to trace the other half of the football.

Following the manufacturer's directions, fuse the traced webbing to the wrong side of the brown fabric piece. Cut out the football, using the traced line on the webbing as a cutting line.

Apply the remaining webbing to the red and white solid fabrics.

Peel away the paper backing on the back of the brown fabric to fuse the football onto a 9-inch white square. Cut away the white fabric around the football, leaving about ¼ inch of white around it.

continued

Center and fuse the football onto the 50-yard line of the field.

Machine-appliqué the football in place, sewing around the raw edges of both brown and white fabrics; stitch details.

Follow manufacturer's instructions for the fabric paint to stencil numbers on each yard line. Stencil the bottom of each number 1½ inches from the edge of the fabric.

Stitching the end zones
Personalize the quilt by appliquéing a child's name, initials, or a favorite team name in the end zones. Use a purchased stencil (or make your own) to draw letters on the red fabric.

Cut out the red letters and fuse them to the surface of the remaining white fabric. Cut around each letter, leaving ¼ inch of white around each one, in the same manner as the football. Fuse the letters onto the green end-zone pieces; appliqué letters in place.

Stitch the completed end zones onto the playing field. Topstitch a 22½-inch-long piece of white ribbon directly over each seam.

Adding the sidelines
Piece tan sideline strips to make two strips 52½ inches long for the sides. Cut two strips 27½ inches long for the ends.

Stitch the side strips onto the field section. Topstitch a 57½-inch-long ribbon over each seam. Sew the shorter tan strips across the ends. Topstitch a 22½-inch-long ribbon atop each seam, tucking the ends of the ribbon under to square them up with the sides.

Stitching the stadium sections
Note: Refer to quilt assembly diagram, *right,* for guidance in assembling the stadium sections.

Sew a gray aisle strip onto both 12½-inch-long sides of one red print stadium piece. Join a blue fabric piece onto the gray sides of the unit.

Add a gray strip onto both ends of the blue pieces. Complete the row with a red block at each end.

Repeat to make the opposite row of the stadium sections. Sew the assembled strips onto the sides of the center field unit.

Stitch the remaining gray aisle strips onto the short sides of both

blue end-zone pieces. Complete the end rows with a green corner block on both ends.

Sew the end-zone strips onto opposite ends of the quilt top.

Quilting and finishing
Divide the backing fabric into two 62-inch-long pieces. Sew the two panels together side by side.

Sandwich the batting between the backing and quilt top; baste the layers together. Trim batting and backing to within 2 inches of each side of the quilt top.

Sewing through all layers, use white thread to topstitch each of the marked 5-yard lines.

Topstitch lines in each stadium section perpendicular to the aisles, spaced 2 inches apart.

A helmet is quilted in each corner block of the quilt. A full-size pattern for the helmet is given, *opposite.* Quilt the helmet by hand or by machine.

Cut approximately 270 inches of 2½-inch-wide red binding. See page 79 for tips on making and applying binding.

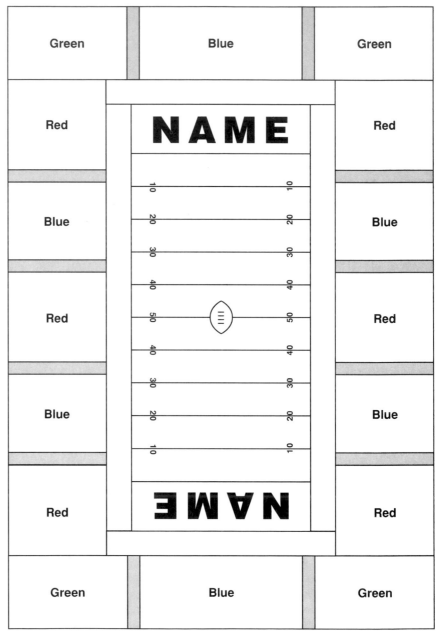

FOOTBALL QUILT ASSEMBLY DIAGRAM

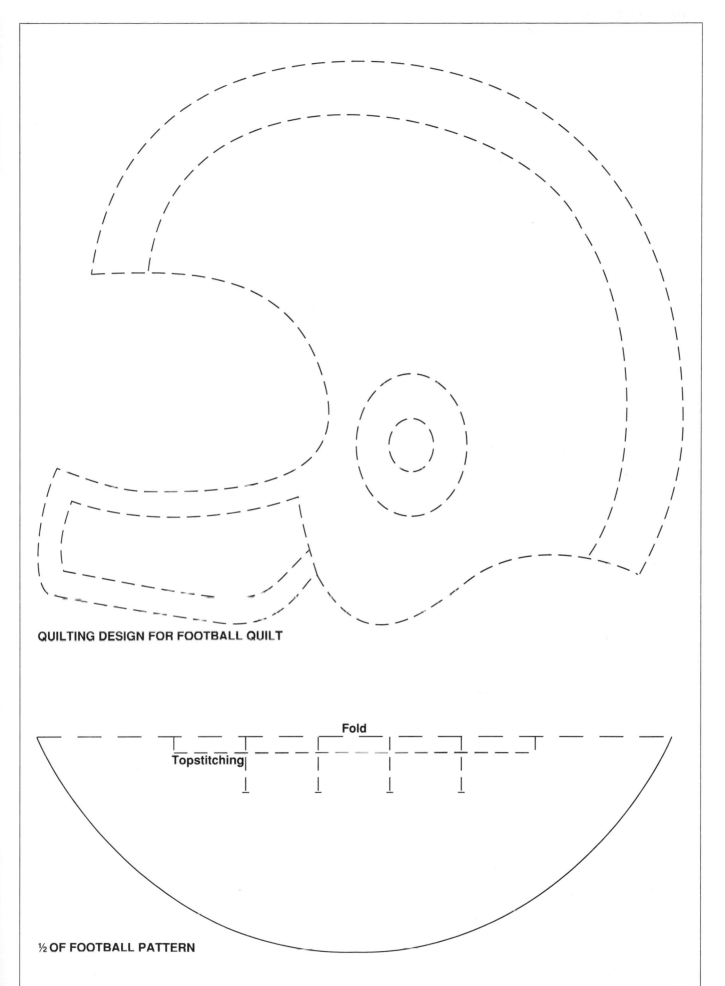

QUILTING DESIGN FOR FOOTBALL QUILT

Fold

Topstitching

½ OF FOOTBALL PATTERN

Rocket Power Quilt

Shown on page 36.

The finished quilt measures approximately 58x72 inches. Each block measures 8x10 inches.

MATERIALS
1¾ yards of black print fabric for sashing and borders
1¾ yards of muslin
Twenty-five 4½x6½-inch plaid fabrics for rockets
Twenty-five 3x9-inch coordinating print fabrics for rockets
Four 3x9-inch dark print fabrics for corner stars
7-inch square of tan fabric for corner stars
1 yard of plaid fabric for binding
4⅜ yards of backing fabric
72x90-inch quilt batting
Template material
Acrylic ruler
Rotary cutter and mat

INSTRUCTIONS
The rocket quilt is assembled in five rows of five blocks each, with sashing strips between blocks. Pieced star blocks highlight the corners of the 6-inch-wide border.

Cutting the fabrics
Make templates for pieces A, B, D, and F from the patterns, *opposite.* (See tips on making templates on page 78.) Pieces C and E can be cut using a ruler and rotary cutter as described here. Refer to the block assembly diagrams, *right* and *far right,* while cutting.

Cut a 5x48-inch strip down one side of the muslin, then cut a 5x37-inch strip from the remaining piece. From these two strips, cut sixty-six 2½-inch C squares.

Cut a 6x37-inch muslin strip; mark and cut 25 B triangles.

For the D pieces, cut a 37-inch square of muslin. Cut the square into 13 lengthwise strips, each 2½x37 inches. Fold each strip in half and cut through two layers to obtain one D and one D reversed from each cut. Cut 25 *each* of D and D reversed.

Set aside one 7-inch muslin square for the star blocks. From the remaining muslin, cut 50 A triangles.

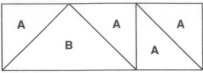

FIGURE 1

Referring to Figure 1, *above,* position templates on each print rocket fabric. Cut four of A and one of B from each fabric.

For the corner stars, cut four of A and one 2½-inch C square from each 3x9-inch dark print fabric.

The 7-inch squares of muslin and tan fabrics are also for the star blocks. Cut 16 F triangles from *each* square as shown in Figure 2, *below.*

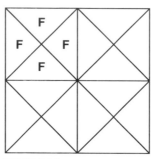

FIGURE 2

From the black print fabric, cut two 6½x61-inch border strips, two 6½x48-inch border strips, and four 3x48-inch strips for the horizontal sashing. From the remaining black fabric, cut twenty 2x10½-inch sashing strips.

Making the rocket block
Note: For ease in quilting, press seams toward the dark fabric except where noted. For each block,

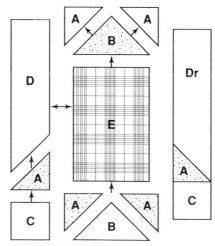

ROCKET BLOCK ASSEMBLY DIAGRAM

select four A triangles and one B triangle from a print fabric that coordinates with the E piece.

Refer to the block assembly diagram *bottom left* as you make each block. The rocket block is assembled in three vertical sections that are joined to complete the block.

To begin the center unit, sew a muslin A triangle onto both short sides of the print B triangle; press seams. Repeat for the second ABA unit, sewing two print A triangles onto the muslin B triangle.

Sew the ABA units onto opposite ends of the E piece as shown; press the joining seams toward the plaid fabric.

For the side sections, stitch a print A triangle to both the D and D reversed pieces as shown. Sew a muslin C square to the end of each A piece. Join side sections to center unit to complete the block.

Make 25 rocket blocks.

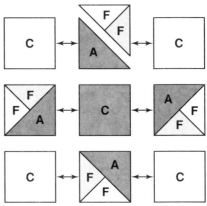

STAR BLOCK ASSEMBLY DIAGRAM

Making the star corner block
Refer to the Star Block Assembly Diagram, *above,* as you sew each block.

Stitch each muslin F triangle to a tan fabric F triangle as shown. Press the seam allowances toward the tan fabric.

Sew each FF triangle onto a dark print A triangle as shown; press the seam allowance toward the A triangle.

For each block, select four FFA pieced units, one print C square, and four muslin C squares. Assemble three horizontal rows as shown in the assembly diagram. Matching seam lines carefully, join rows to complete the block.

Make four star blocks.

Assembling the quilt top

Lay out the rocket blocks in five horizontal rows, with five blocks in each row.

Assemble each row, sewing a 2x10½-inch sashing strip between each block; press seam allowances toward the sashing.

Join the rows by stitching a 3x48-inch sashing strip between each row. Trim sashing strips even with the rocket block rows.

Stitch the 61-inch-long border strips onto the sides of the quilt top; press seams toward borders. Trim borders even with quilt top.

Sew a star block onto one end of each remaining border strip. Before sewing a block onto the opposite ends, however, compare the length of each border strip to the top and bottom edges of the quilt top. Trim excess border fabric, but be sure to leave a seam allowance for the star block.

Join remaining star blocks to border strips, then sew completed strips to the top and bottom edges of the quilt top.

Quilting and finishing

Cut the backing fabric into two 78-inch-long pieces. Use a ½-inch seam allowance to stitch the center seam. Trim seam allowance to ¼ inch and press to one side.

Layer the backing, batting, and quilt top; baste the three layers together. Quilt as desired. The quilt pictured on page 36 has outline quilting on the stars and rocket fins, vertical lines on the plaid rocket bodies, and a variety of stars quilted on the borders.

When quilting is complete, remove basting and trim the batting and backing even with the quilt top.

Refer to page 79 for tips on making and applying binding.

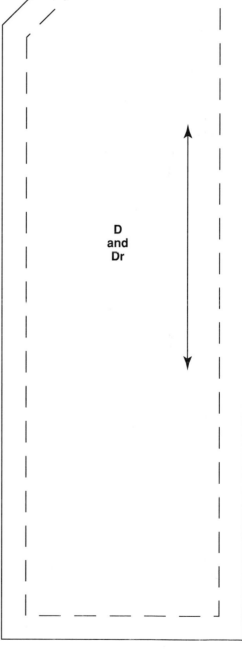

ROCKET POWER QUILT PATTERNS

49

CHILD'S PLAY

◆ ◆ ◆

With its ever-rich interplay of color and artful pattern, patchwork brings warmth and personality to a youngster's world. Choose traditional hues, work with a palette of the child's favorite shades, or dip into your remnants to piece a scrap quilt of many colors. Today's exciting fabrics provide endless possibilities for making a quilt with the one-of-a-kind cachet that children love. The captivating patchwork projects in this chapter are sure to be today's delight and tomorrow's childhood treasures.

Center stage in the youthful universe, *right,* is a star-bright Starry Sky Quilt to make your child's wish for a fantasy space come true. Its heavenly hues and celestial theme may inspire a roomful of imaginative patchwork accents—from toss pillows to a baby doll on a star-studded cloud.

Traditional pieced star blocks twinkle against the luminous "sky" background of a swirling print fabric and cloudlike quilting.

The quilt measures approximately 68x88 inches, and each block is 10 inches square.

The quilt instructions begin on page 56.

Watching over your little one's slumber, the angelic Bedpost Baby Doll, *opposite,* is all dressed up in a matching patchwork star block. With her mop of golden curls and sweet details, she's a 16-inch-tall huggable playmate.

Instructions and patterns for the doll begin on page 57.

Long ago, girls learned to sew by making diminutive doll quilts from snippets of fabric and thread. Today's dollies need little quilts, too, and charming miniatures hold a special spot in the stitcher's heart.

The 16¾x21-inch doll quilt, *above*, draws appeal from pastel prints and pieced blocks in a daylily motif. Each block is 3 inches square and set on the diagonal with alternating plain blocks. Instructions begin on page 60.

Adorable for the bed or a wall display, the ruffled bows patchwork, *opposite*, is a scrap quilt that works magic with assorted buttons for tacking at the sashing squares.

The quilt instructions begin on page 62.

On-the-grow young women will be delighted by the light-hearted Sister's Choice Quilt, *left,* a stylized adaptation of the ever-popular patchwork star motif that is just right for any age.

Stitched with a fresh bouquet of pastel and garden-green fabrics, this quilt will inspire accessories for a whole bedroom scheme. For a growing boy, pick lively primaries or his favorite colors to create a different look.

The 63x86-inch quilt combines 24 prints with a solid fabric that links the merry mix together.

Endearing scrap quilts such as this one exude singular appeal because each is unique. The quiltmaker's eye and imagination, juxtaposing fabric colors and patterns, make all the difference   and all the fun.

To speed the project along, the instructions include tips on a quick-piecing technique and on tying the quilt with perle cotton or washable yarn.

The star blocks are each 10 inchcs squarc, and each of the 24 blocks uses a different print fabric. The star points may be sewn by the quick-piecing or traditional method.

Set in a sea of multicolored sashing, simple four-patch blocks, each made of four randomly chosen fabrics, are used for sashing squares. The dominant solid fabric is repeated in the design-framing border, and the prairie-point edging reprises the myriad print fabrics.

Instructions for the Sister's Choice Quilt begin on page 64.

Starry Sky Quilt

Shown on pages 50 and 51.

The finished quilt measures approximately 68x88 inches. Each block is 10 inches square.

MATERIALS
5 yards of "sky" fabric
 for setting squares, borders, and binding
1¾ yards *each* of solid white and purple print fabrics
5⅝ yards of backing fabric
81x96-inch precut quilt batting
Template material

INSTRUCTIONS
This star quilt looks heavenly with the swirling purple and turquoise print skylike fabric that we used, but it could have a more down-to-earth appeal with different fabrics. For example, you might try a rainbow print with stars of different primary colors.

The quilt consists of 18 pieced star blocks, alternating with 17 plain blocks of sky fabric. The blocks are joined in seven rows of five blocks each.

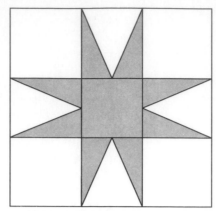

STARRY SKY BLOCK

Cutting the fabrics
Refer to page 78 for tips on preparing and using templates for patchwork. To match the triangle points precisely, we recommend using a window template to mark sewing *and* cutting lines on the fabric. Make templates for patterns A and B, *below*.

From the purple print fabric, cut seventeen 3½x42-inch strips. Set aside seven strips for the inner border. Use two strips to cut eighteen 3½-inch squares for the star centers.

From the remaining eight purple strips, cut 72 rectangles, each 3½x4¼ inches. Cut two of Pattern A from each rectangle—first cut 72 of Pattern A from 36 of the rectangles, then turn the template over (faceup) and cut 72 of Pattern A reversed from the 36 remaining rectangles.

From the white fabric, cut six 3½x42-inch strips. From these strips, cut seventy-two 3½-inch squares for the block patchwork.

Cut six 4x42-inch strips from the remaining white fabric. Cut 72 of Pattern B, cutting 12 from each strip.

From the sky fabric, cut eight 6½x42-inch border strips and eight 2¼x42-inch binding strips. From the remaining sky fabric, cut seventeen 10½-inch squares.

Piecing the star block
Note: Throughout the quilt assembly, press seam allowances toward the darker fabric. Press each seam before proceeding to the next step.

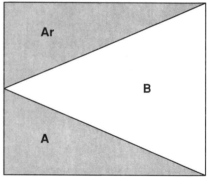

FIGURE 1

With right sides together, sew one A piece and one A reversed piece to opposite sides of each B triangle as shown in Figure 1, *above*. If the sewing lines are marked on each piece, put a pin through both layers of fabric to correctly align the corners.

Stitch 72 of these pieced units.

Referring to the block diagram, *top left*, join the pieced units with the squares of white and purple fabric to assemble three horizontal rows for each block as follows.

Sew one pieced unit to two opposite sides of the purple center square. Position the pieced units so that the wide ends of the purple star points are next to the

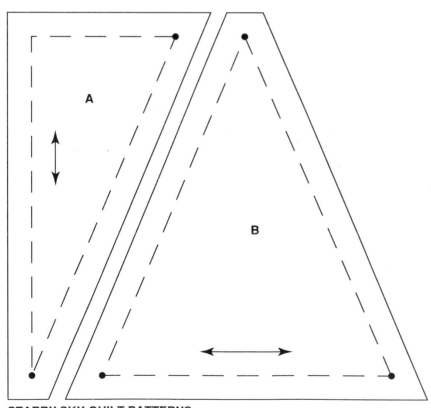

STARRY SKY QUILT PATTERNS

square. Press seam allowances away from the center square.

Stitch a white square to both purple sides of two pieced units; press the seam allowances toward the purple fabric.

Matching the center seam lines carefully, join the three horizontal rows to complete the block. Make 18 star blocks.

Assembling the quilt
Assemble seven horizontal rows of five blocks each, alternating star blocks with the plain blocks of sky fabric. Make four rows with star blocks at both ends and three rows with plain blocks at both ends. Press the seam allowances toward the plain blocks.

Join the seven rows, alternating star and plain blocks.

Adding the borders
Cut one 42-inch-long purple border strip in half, making two 21-inch-long strips. Stitch each of these short strips end to end with one 42-inch-long border strip.

Sew one assembled border to the bottom edge of the quilt top. Press the seam allowance toward the border; trim excess border fabric even with the sides of the quilt. Sew the second border strip to the opposite end of the quilt top in the same manner.

Join two remaining purple border strips to make one border long enough for each side of the quilt top. Sew borders to the sides in the same manner.

Piece two border strips of sky fabric for each end of the quilt. Join these to the quilt top in the same manner as the purple border. Add the excess fabric from these short borders to the remaining strips of sky fabric to make a border long enough for each side. Stitch borders to sides.

Quilting and finishing
Layer the quilt top, batting, and backing; baste the three layers together. Quilt a free-form pattern of clouds over the surface of the quilt top.

When the quilting is complete, remove basting. Refer to page 79 for tips on making and applying straight-grain binding.

Bedpost Baby Doll

Shown on pages 51 and 58.

The doll measures 16½ inches tall, not including the hanger.

MATERIALS
⅜ yard *each* of solid white and turquoise print fabrics for the doll's dress and ruffle
6x10-inch piece of purple print fabric for the star patchwork
9-inch square of flesh-colored fabric
Polyester filling
½ yard of ½-inch-wide purple grosgrain ribbon for hanger
Two skeins of gold embroidery floss for hair
Six ½-inch-diameter star sequins
Red crayon or pressed blush makeup for cheek coloring
Brown fabric marker for eyes
2-inch square of cardboard
Template material
Glue gun or crafts glue (optional)

INSTRUCTIONS
We used the "starry sky" block for the doll's dress to coordinate with the quilt, but you can substi-

tute any 10-inch (finished size) quilt block or a solid square of a coordinating fabric.

Note: A ¼-inch seam allowance is used throughout the construction of the doll.

Cutting the fabrics
Make templates for patterns A and B, *opposite*. Make a template or a tissue pattern for the cloud pattern, *below*, as well as for the sleeve and body patterns on pages 58 and 59. If you prefer, you can trace these patterns directly onto the white fabric.

From the purple print fabric, cut four of Pattern A, four of Pattern A reversed, and one 3½-inch square for the patchwork star.

From the white fabric, cut two clouds and two sleeves. From the remaining white fabric, cut four 4-inch squares and four of Pattern B for the patchwork.

continued

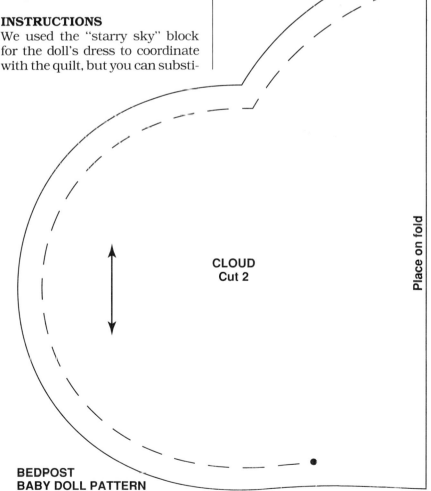

CLOUD
Cut 2

Place on fold

BEDPOST
BABY DOLL PATTERN

Cut two body pieces from the flesh-colored fabric.

For the dress, cut two 10½-inch squares of turquoise print fabric, then cut three 4x20-inch strips for the ruffle.

Making the doll body
With right sides facing, sew the two body pieces together. Leave the straight bottom edge open as indicated on the pattern, *below*.

Clip the seam allowance at the neck as indicated on the pattern. Turn the body right side out; stuff it with polyester filling until firm.

Turn under the raw edge at the bottom edge of the body; hand-sew the opening closed.

Add dot eyes as indicated on the pattern with a fabric marker or embroidery, if you prefer. Rub a little crayon on the face to give the doll rosy cheeks.

BEDPOST BABY DOLL

Making the doll's hair
Use the 2-inch square of cardboard as a measuring guide to make the doll's hair.

Wrap embroidery floss around the cardboard square 11 times. Slip the wrapped floss off the cardboard; tie a piece of matching thread or floss around the bundle to secure it. Make 12 floss bundles in this manner.

Glue or hand-sew the bundles to the top of the doll's head, centering them over the body seam. Fluff the loops by slightly separating the strands of floss.

Making the doll's dress
PATCHWORK: Refer to the directions for piecing the star block on page 56. Make four pieced triangle units as described. Join the triangle units with plain squares of the white and purple fabrics to complete one block as shown in the block diagram on page 56.

Stitch the 10½-inch squares of turquoise fabric onto opposite sides of the star block, making a long rectangle. Press seam allowances away from the patchwork.

RUFFLE: Seam the three ruffle strips together end to end; press the seam allowances open.

On one long edge of the ruffle strip, press ½ inch back to the wrong side. Turn the hem back again, enclosing the raw edge in a hem. Topstitch the hem in place.

Baste a loose gathering stitch ¼ inch from the remaining raw edge of the ruffle strip. Gather the ruffle to fit the long bottom edge of the dress rectangle.

continued

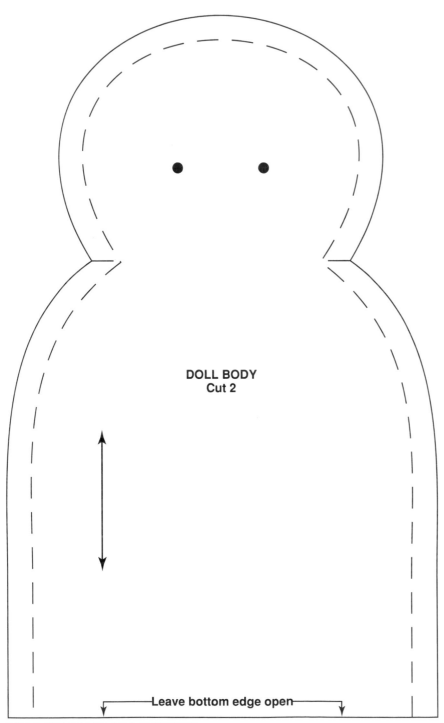

DOLL BODY
Cut 2

Leave bottom edge open

BEDPOST BABY DOLL PATTERN

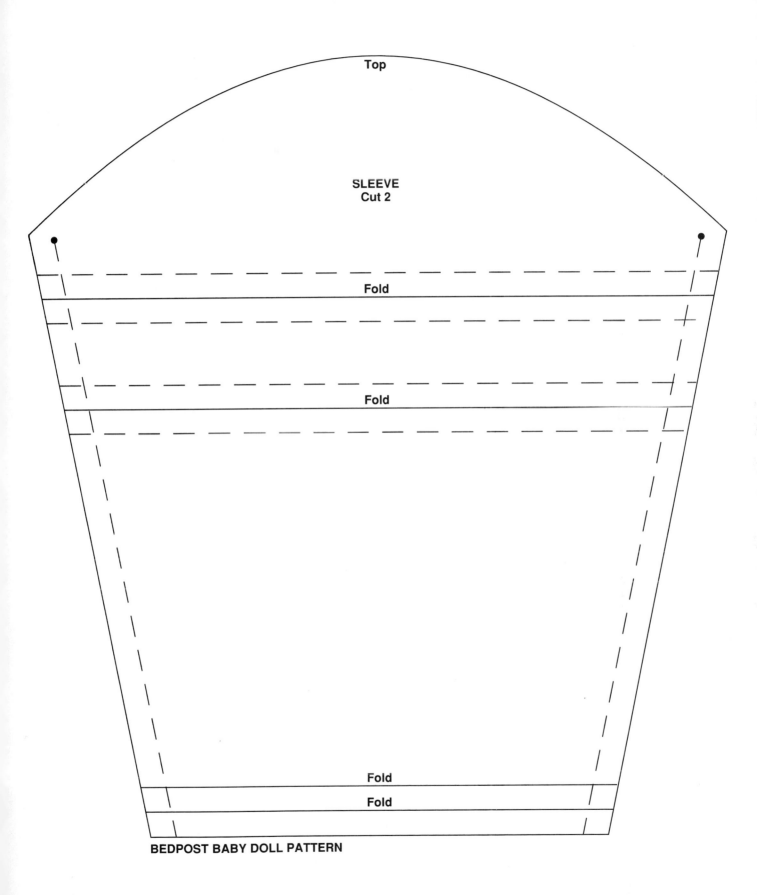

Top

SLEEVE
Cut 2

Fold

Fold

Fold

Fold

BEDPOST BABY DOLL PATTERN

Matching right sides and raw edges, sew the ruffle to one long edge of the dress rectangle. Press the seam allowances away from the ruffle; topstitch through the seam allowances at the bottom of the dress.

DRESS: Turn under a ¼-inch hem at the top edge of the dress; press. Sew a double line of basting stitches along the top of the dress through the folded hem.

Bring the raw edges of the turquoise squares together, matching right sides; stitch the center back seam of the dress.

Insert the doll body into the dress; gather the top edge until the dress fits snugly at the doll's neck. Tie the gathering threads in a knot at the back to secure them.

Making the sleeves
With right sides facing, fold each sleeve on the lines indicated on the pattern. Using a contrasting thread color, topstitch ¼ inch from each fold to sew the tucks in place. Press both tucks toward the sleeve bottom.

Turn ¼ inch of fabric to the wrong side at the bottom edge of each sleeve piece. Turn the folded fabric over again, concealing the raw edge in the hem. Topstitch the hem in place.

With right sides facing, stitch the sleeve sides together, sewing from the hemmed bottom edge to the dot marked on the pattern. Turn the sleeve right side out.

With contrasting thread, hand-sew a row of gathering stitches just below the hem of each sleeve. Pull the gathers tight and tie off the thread, creating a ruffle at the end of each sleeve.

Turn under a ¼-inch seam allowance at the curved top edge of the sleeve. Hand-sew a gathering stitch through the seam allowance. Fill the sleeve with a small amount of polyester filling, then pull the gathering stitches tight to close the top of the sleeve. Tie off the thread with a knot.

Glue or hand-sew the completed sleeves to the sides of the dress just below the neck, positioning the center side seam of the sleeve against the body of the doll.

Making the cloud and hanger
Stitch the cloud pieces together, leaving a small opening for turning. Clip the seam allowance at the corners as indicated on the pattern. Turn the cloud right side out through the opening.

Lightly stuff the cloud with polyester filling. Hand-stitch the opening closed.

Stitch the star sequins in place on the cloud, sewing through all layers to create a slightly tufted appearance. Center the cloud at the back of the doll's head; glue or stitch it in place.

Tie a knot in both ends of the grosgrain ribbon. Positioning the knots at the bottom corners of the cloud, glue or stitch the ribbon onto the back of the cloud to make the hanger.

Daylily Doll Quilt

Shown on page 52.

The finished doll quilt measures 16¾x21 inches. Each daylily block is 3 inches square.

MATERIALS
½ yard *each* of rose print and light blue dotted fabrics
⅛ yard *each* of blue print, pink solid, and dark blue print fabrics
18x24-inch piece of quilt batting
Template material
Acrylic ruler
Rotary cutter and mat

INSTRUCTIONS
This doll-size quilt is made of twelve 3-inch daylily blocks set on the diagonal with alternate plain blocks of blue dotted fabric.

Cutting the fabrics
Refer to page 78 for tips on making templates for patchwork. Prepare templates for patterns A and B, *opposite*.

Cut an 18x24-inch piece of light blue dotted fabric for backing. From the remaining 18-inch square, cut one strip 5½x16½ inches and two 3-inch squares.

Cut both the 3-inch squares in half diagonally to obtain four corner setting triangles. For the side

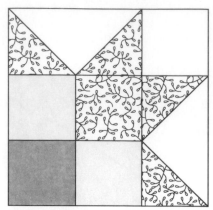

DAYLILY BLOCK

triangles, cut the 5½x16½-inch strip into three 5½-inch squares; cut each of these squares in quarters diagonally, as shown in Figure 1, *below*. This makes 12 setting triangles, two more than are necessary for this doll quilt.

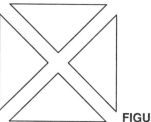

FIGURE 1

From the remaining light blue dotted fabric, cut six 3½-inch setting squares.

From the rose print fabric, cut three 2x42-inch strips. Set two strips aside for binding; cut 48 B triangles from the third strip.

From the remaining rose print fabric, cut two 2½x20-inch strips and two 2½x24-inch strips for the border. These border strips are slightly longer than needed; they will be cut to exact size after they are sewn to the quilt top.

For the C squares, cut twelve 1½-inch squares from *each* of the dark blue, rose print, and pink solid fabrics. Cut 24 C squares from the blue print fabric.

Cut 24 A triangles from the pink solid fabric.

Making the daylily block
Refer to the Block Assembly Diagram, *opposite*, to piece the daylily block.

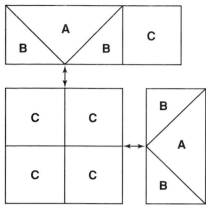

BLOCK ASSEMBLY DIAGRAM

Each block is composed of two A triangles of pink solid fabric, four rose print B triangles, one C square *each* of pink solid, dark blue, and rose print fabrics, and two C squares of blue print fabric.

Stitch two B triangles onto the sides of each A triangle as shown. Make two BAB units for each block; press the seam allowances toward the B triangles.

Sew the pink solid C square onto the right side of one BAB unit, as shown.

Stitch a blue print C square to one side of the remaining dark blue and rose print squares; press the seam allowance toward the blue print fabric. Join the two rows into a larger square, positioning the dark blue square in the outside corner of the block.

Sew the BAB unit onto one side of the pieced center unit, positioning the units as shown in the Block Assembly Diagram. Stitch the remaining BABC unit to the top edge to complete the block.

Make 12 daylily blocks.

Assembling the quilt top
Join the daylily blocks with setting squares and triangles to make the diagonal rows indicated by the red lines in the quilt diagram, *above right*. Join the rows as shown. Add the corner triangles to complete the quilt top.

Sew the shorter border strips to the top and bottom edges of the assembled quilt. Trim the border

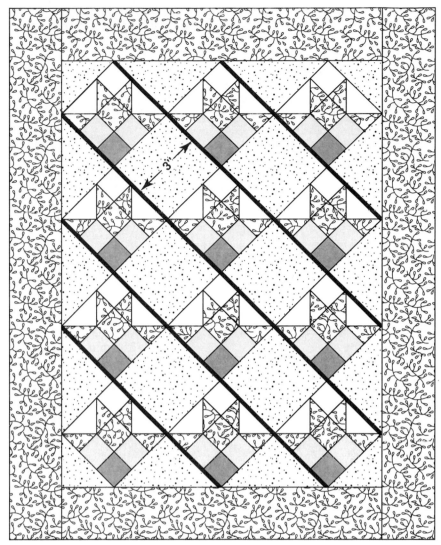

DAYLILY QUILT ASSEMBLY DIAGRAM

fabric even with the sides of the quilt; press the seam allowances toward the border. Add the longer borders to the sides in the same manner.

Quilting and finishing
Mark desired quilting design on the quilt top. The quilt shown has quilting "in the ditch" (along the seam lines) on the pieced blocks and an outline of the patchwork motif in the setting squares.

Layer the quilt top, batting, and backing; baste the three layers together. Quilt as desired.

When the quilting is complete, remove basting. Refer to page 79 for tips on making and applying the binding, using the remaining two 2x42-inch strips of rose fabric. Make approximately 80 inches of straight-grain binding.

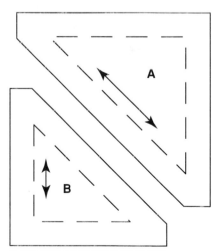

DAYLILY QUILT PATTERNS

61

Buttons and Bows Crib Quilt

Shown on page 53.

The finished quilt measures approximately 46¼ × 53¾ inches, plus a 1¾-inch ruffle. Each bow block is 6¼ inches square.

MATERIALS
3¼ yards of printed muslin for sashing and backing fabric
1⅛ yards of print fabric for the ruffle
⅛ yard *each* of 21 different solid fabrics for the bows
One 3x14-inch scrap *each* of 42 coordinating print fabrics for block backgrounds
1⅜ yards of 60-inch-wide quilt batting
56 assorted large buttons
Template material

INSTRUCTIONS
This quilt consists of 42 bow blocks. Each block is made with a different pair of scrap fabrics. The bow is a solid fabric, stitched against a background of print

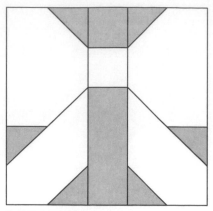

BOW BLOCK

fabric. Muslin sashing separates the blocks; squares of solid fabric scraps divide the sashing at the block corners.

Cutting the fabrics
Refer to page 78 for tips on making templates for patchwork. Prepare templates from patterns A, B, and C, *opposite.*

Cut each solid fabric in half to obtain two 4½x21-inch pieces. Match each of the 42 solid pieces with one of the print fabrics to make 42 fabric pairs, one for each bow block.

For each solid fabric, cut one 1¾-inch square, two of Pattern A, and one of Pattern C; then turn the C template over to cut one of Pattern C reversed.

From each of the background print fabrics, cut one 1¾x4¼-inch piece, one 1¾-inch square, and six B triangles for each block.

Cut the muslin into two 58-inch lengths. From one panel, cut two 5x58-inch strips; set these aside with the remaining whole panel for the backing.

From the remaining 32x58-inch muslin piece, cut 97 sashing strips, each 1¾ × 6¾ inches.

From the remaining scraps of solid fabrics, cut fifty-six 1¾-inch squares for the sashing.

Piecing the bow blocks
Piece the block in three vertical sections as shown in the block assembly diagram, *opposite.*

Begin by stitching a B triangle onto two sides of the A piece as shown. Sew another B triangle onto the short diagonal edge of the C piece. Press seam allowances toward the darker fabric. Complete the section by stitching

Tying Your Quilts

Tying is a quick and easy alternative to hand quilting, and it is an appropriate and useful finish for a quilt that will get a lot of wear and tear. Save your fine hand stitching for the quilt that will be cared for and treasured.

For a more creative approach, sew buttons or other colorful ornaments through the quilt layers. This is sometimes called tufting.

The best material for tying is perle cotton or sport-weight yarn. A tie is sewn through all three layers of the quilt—backing, batting, and quilt top—and knotted on the surface of the quilt top.

Thread a large-eyed needle with two 18-inch-long strands of perle cotton or one strand of yarn.

1 From the right side, push the threaded needle through all layers of the quilt. Pull the needle through, leaving a 2½-inch-long tail of thread on the surface. Push the needle back to the quilt top about ⅛ inch from the first tail.

2 Push the needle back down in the first hole.

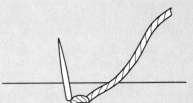

3 Bring the needle up again through the second hole. Cut the thread, leaving a 2½-inch-long tail.

4 Tie the clipped threads in a square knot close to the surface of the quilt top. To avoid puckers in the quilt, do not knot the threads too tightly.

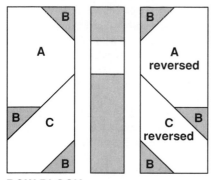

**BOW BLOCK
ASSEMBLY DIAGRAM**

the two units together along the diagonal edge.

Repeat the process with the A and C reversed pieces to make the opposite side of the block.

For the center strip of the block, join a 1¾-inch square of the print fabric with one square of the solid fabric. Complete the strip by joining the 4¼-inch-long print fabric piece to the opposite side of the solid square.

Stitch the three sections together to finish one block.

Make 42 bow blocks.

Assembling the quilt top

Arrange the blocks in seven horizontal rows, with six blocks in each row.

Join the blocks in each row, stitching a sashing strip between each block. Sew a sashing strip to the remaining block edges at each end of the row. Press seam allowances toward the sashing.

Make horizontal sashing rows by joining six sashing strips and seven sashing squares. Begin and end each row with a square, and alternate the squares with sashing strips. Make eight rows of horizontal sashing.

Starting with a sashing row, sew rows of sashing and blocks together to complete the quilt top.

Finishing

RUFFLE: Cut the ruffle fabric into nine 4x42-inch strips. Sew all the strips together end to end; press the seam allowances open.

Fold the strip in half lengthwise, wrong sides together, and press. Topstitch a loose gathering stitch ¼ inch from the raw edge of the strip.

Gather the ruffle strip to fit around the quilt top. Matching the raw edges of the ruffle with the edge of the quilt top, pin the ruffle in place. Overlap the ends where they meet. Baste the ruffle in place; remove pins.

BACKING: Stitch one 5-inch-wide muslin strip to each side of the 42x58-inch muslin panel; press the seam allowances open.

Cut the batting to the same size as the quilt top. Baste the batting to the wrong side of the quilt top. Pin the ruffle flat on the quilt top.

Center the quilt on the backing fabric, right sides together. Stitch a ¼-inch seam around the edge of the quilt top, sewing through all layers. Leave an 8- to 10-inch opening in the middle of one side.

Turn the quilt through the opening; remove pins from ruffle; slip-stitch the opening closed.

TYING: Baste all three layers of the quilt together.

Finish the quilt by sewing a button in place on each sashing square, stitching through all layers. If you prefer, use perle cotton to tie the crib quilt. Refer to the tips on tying, *opposite*.

When tying is complete, carefully remove all basting.

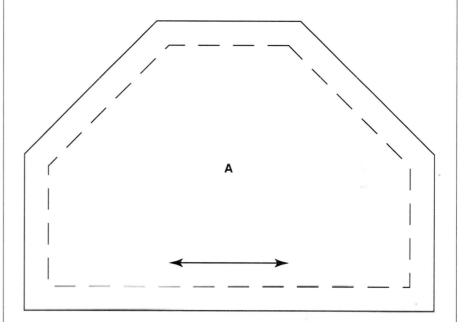

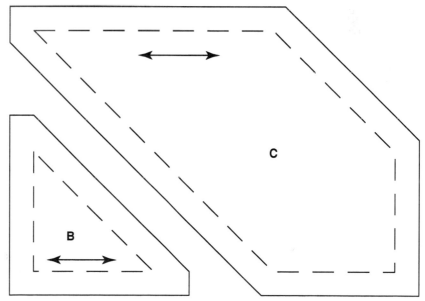

BUTTONS AND BOWS CRIB QUILT PATTERNS

63

Sister's Choice Quilt

Shown on pages 54 and 55.

The finished quilt measures approximately 63x86 inches. Each block is 10 inches square.

MATERIALS
3¼ yards of green fabric for blocks, borders, and binding
2½ yards of muslin for blocks and middle border
¼ yard *each* of 24 pastel print fabrics for blocks, sashing, and prairie points
5¼ yards of backing fabric
72x90-inch precut quilt batt
Two skeins of perle cotton and a large-eyed needle for tying
Acrylic ruler
Rotary cutter and mat

INSTRUCTIONS
These directions describe a technique for quick-pieced triangle-squares. The fabric designated for quick piecing is large enough to cut individual triangles for traditional piecing, if desired.

Cutting the fabrics
From the green fabric, cut eight 1¾x42-inch strips for binding and fourteen 3x42¼-inch strips for the borders.

Cut eight 2½x42-inch strips of green fabric; cut sixteen 2½-inch squares from each strip until you have a total of 120 squares.

From the remaining green fabric, cut four 18-inch squares for the quick-pieced triangles.

Cut seven 3x42-inch strips of muslin for the middle border. For the block patchwork, cut twelve 2½x42-inch muslin strips; cut these into 2½-inch squares for a total of 192 squares.

Cut four 18-inch squares from the remaining muslin for the triangle-squares.

From *each* print fabric, cut four 2½-inch squares for the blocks.

Cut five or six 1½x10½-inch sashing strips from each print fabric to obtain a total of 116 strips. Cut 140 assorted sashing squares, each 1½ inches square.

Cut the remaining print fabrics into 3-inch squares for the edging of prairie points. Cut at least 150 squares of assorted fabrics.

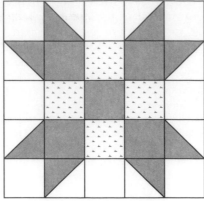

SISTER'S CHOICE BLOCK

Making the triangle-squares
Note: Refer to the tips on page 41 for more complete instructions on quick-pieced triangle-squares.

Each Sister's Choice block includes eight triangle-squares; each square consists of one green triangle and one muslin triangle (see the block diagram, *above*).

For traditional piecing, mark the fabrics designated for triangle-squares as described in Step 1 and illustrated in Figure 1, *below;* then cut the individual triangles apart before any sewing is done.

● Referring to Figure 1, *below,* mark a 5x5-square grid of 2⅞-inch squares on the wrong side of an 18-inch muslin square.

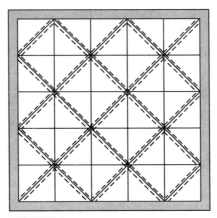

FIGURE 1

● With right sides facing, place the muslin square (marked side up) atop a matching square of green fabric; pin the fabrics together at the corners.

Stitch ¼ inch from both sides of each *diagonal* line (indicated by the red lines in Figure 1).

● Cut the grid into 50 triangle-squares, cutting on all the marked lines. Press seam allowances toward the green fabric.

Complete four grids of triangle-squares. This will result in eight more triangle-squares than the 192 needed for the Sister's Choice blocks; discard any squares that are misshapen or distorted.

Assembling the blocks
Each block is made by joining twenty-five 2½-inch squares into five rows of five squares each, as shown in the Block Assembly Diagram, *below.*

For each block, select eight triangle-squares, five green squares, eight squares of muslin, and four squares of one print fabric.

Assemble the blocks in rows, positioning the fabrics as shown in the diagram. Matching seam lines carefully, join the rows to complete the block.

Make 24 Sister's Choice blocks, using a different print fabric in each block.

Assembling the quilt top
Select four 1½-inch squares of assorted print fabrics at random; sew the squares together in pairs, then join the pairs to complete a four-patch sashing square. Make 35 sashing squares.

On the floor or a large table, lay out all the Sister's Choice blocks in six horizontal rows of four blocks each. Position a four-patch sashing square between blocks at each corner.

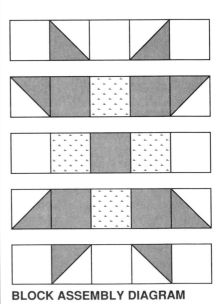

BLOCK ASSEMBLY DIAGRAM

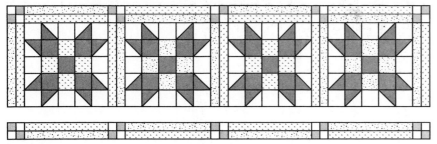

FIGURE 2

Fill the spaces between blocks and at both ends of each row with sashing strips, surrounding each block with sashing strips of the same fabric.

For the block rows, begin by sewing adjacent sashing strips together; press the seam allowances to one side. Join sashing strips and blocks in a row as shown in Figure 2, *above*. Complete six block rows.

To make the horizontal sashing rows, begin by sewing adjacent sashing strips together. Join the sashing strips and squares in a row as shown in Figure 2. Make seven sashing rows.

Alternating the block rows and sashing rows, join the rows as shown in Figure 2 to complete the quilt assembly.

Adding the borders

Cut one green border strip in half; sew each half strip to a whole strip, end to end, to make one border long enough for each end of the quilt.

Stitch these borders to the top and bottom edges of the assembled quilt top; press seam allowances toward the border. Trim excess border fabric even with the sides of the quilt.

Join two green border strips to make one border long enough for each side. Stitch the side borders onto the quilt top. Press seams; trim excess border fabric.

Repeat this procedure with the muslin strips to add the center border. Add the outside border in the same manner, using the remaining strips of green fabric.

Making the prairie points

Fold each 3-inch square of print fabric in half diagonally, wrong sides together, to make a triangle. Fold the triangle in half again, bringing the points together to form a smaller triangle. Press the prairie point flat.

With the right side of the quilt top facing up, pin the folded triangles around the quilt top, matching the long side of the triangle with the edge of the border as shown in Figure 3, *below*. Position approximately 31 prairie points on each end and 44 on each side. (A few more or less may be needed to accommodate the size of your quilt.) Slightly overlap the triangles.

Machine-baste the triangles in place ¼ inch from the edge.

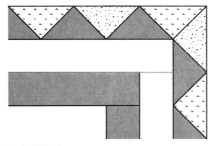

FIGURE 3

Finishing the quilt

Divide the backing fabric into two 2⅛-yard lengths. Stitch the two pieces together side by side; press the seam allowance to one side.

Sandwich the batting between the backing and the quilt top. Baste the three layers together.

TYING: Refer to page 62 for tips on how to tie a quilt.

The quilt shown on pages 54 and 55 is tied with ecru perle cotton. You also can tie with a washable yarn, if you prefer.

In the quilt shown, each block is tied at the corners of the center square and at the tip of each star point. Additional ties are placed at the center of each sashing square, at border corners, and at 6-inch intervals along each border.

BINDING: Piece the green binding strips end to end to make four strips, each long enough to bind one edge of the quilt.

Fold each strip in half, with the wrong sides together, so that it is ⅞ inch wide. Press all four binding strips.

Match the raw edge of the binding with the bottom edge of the quilt, laying the binding atop the basted prairie points. Machine-stitch ¼ inch from the edge as shown in Figure 4, *below,* sewing through all five layers (binding, prairie points, quilt top, batting, and backing).

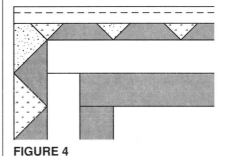

FIGURE 4

Trim the ends of the binding strip even with the sides of the quilt. Turn the folded edge of the binding over to the back of the quilt; hand-sew it in place on the backing fabric. When the binding is turned, the prairie points will stand up in their proper position.

After you've bound the top and bottom edges, repeat the procedure for the sides of the quilt. Turn in the ends of the binding strips to conceal the raw edges.

GREAT QUILTS FOR TEENS

♦ ♦ ♦

Versatile quilts are always a hit with teenagers, because these beauties add warmth and individuality to the bedroom. They also bring a touch of home to a college dorm room or first apartment. For the graduate, a made-with-love quilt is a great gift from a parent or grandparent. In this chapter, you'll find appealing designs to suit a teen's evolving style, from traditional patchwork to contemporary stripes and appliqué.

Among the most treasured heirloom quilts are the appliquéd floral motifs. Our delightful Tulip Garden Quilt, *right,* combines the best of the old and new with contemporary flair and the freshest of colors. These gay blossoms are so pretty, in fact, they'll inspire a bouquet of eye-catching room accents.

With simple shapes and graceful curves, this tulip garden is easily appliquéd by hand or by machine. Our tulips vary in height from 8 inches to 14 inches to add visual interest in this lively garden.

For easy stitching, the quilt top is appliquéd in three sections. After it is assembled, the center section is quilted in a simple grid pattern.

The finished size is approximately 67x88 inches. Instructions begin on page 72.

With bold colors and graphic patterns to please any teenager's truly-today style, these cozy quilts are stitched up in no time with easy-does-it piecing.

Down-home fabric goes contemporary in our Pillow Ticking Quilt, *opposite*, tufted with a multitude of colorful buttons. Alternating the direction of each square's stripes creates an illusion of interwoven lines.

Any color of ticking or striped fabric works well for this 64x92-inch quilt. Instructions begin on page 74.

A kaleidoscope of solid colors and randomly cut strips puts the dazzle in the Stars and Stripes Quilt, *above*. Bound with a flashy star-print fabric, the quilt measures 72x94 inches.

Instructions begin on page 75.

Personality patch-works have long been the signature of artistic quilters who can't resist spicing up time-honored designs with fresh fabrics and imaginative piecing details. Our fetching Pony Express Star Quilt, *right,* is just that—a beautiful twist on tradition.

With a grateful nod to those old-time mailmen, we've named our teen-pleasing quilt for the Pony Express because postage-stamp-size squares of scrap fabric are at the heart of each 12-inch-square star.

Appropriately, this block also is known as the Grandmother's Star; what better or more cherished gift could a grandmother make for a growing grandchild?

In the best of the scrap quilt tradition, this patchwork suc-ceeds with a wealth of randomly placed fabrics. Reds, greens, blues, and earthy colors are sprinkled throughout the blocks and borders. The richer the mix of fabrics, the prettier the quilt; this one delivers the goods with a joyful jumble of small and medium-scale prints, stripes, and plaids.

At the center of each star block is a quartet of basic nine-patch squares made of scrap fabrics. Diverse prints and colors also are used for the star points and joined with a unifying background fabric.

The finished size of the quilt is 68x92 inches. Instructions are on pages 76 and 77.

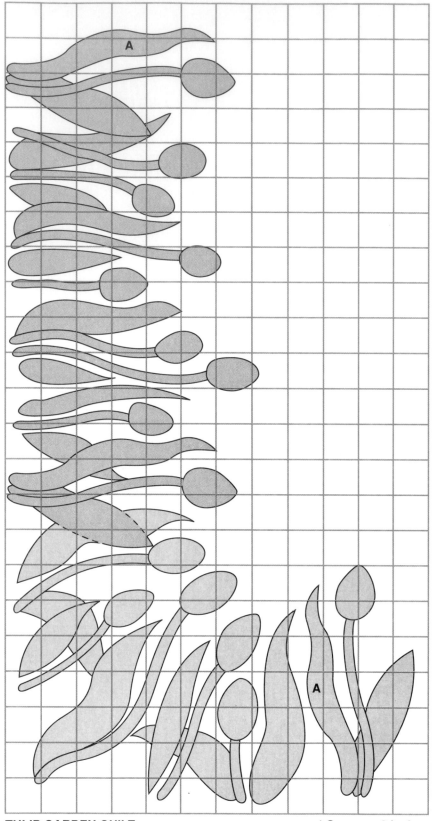

TULIP GARDEN QUILT   **1 Square = 2 Inches**

Tulip Garden Quilt

Shown on pages 66 and 67.

The finished quilt measures approximately 67x88 inches.

MATERIALS
5¼ yards of white and green checked fabric
1⅝ yards *each* of three different shades of solid green fabric for the tulip leaves
¼ yard *each* of red, yellow, orange, purple, light pink, and dark pink fabrics for tulips
1¼ yards of magenta fabric for seventh tulip color and binding
5½ yards of backing fabric
5 yards of paper-backed fusible webbing (for machine appliqué only)
81x96-inch quilt batting
Ruler
Nonpermanent fabric marker
Colored pencils and graph paper
Clear nylon thread (optional for machine quilting)

INSTRUCTIONS
These instructions are given for machine appliqué. If you prefer to appliqué by hand, add 3/16-inch seam allowances to the patterns made from the gridded pattern, *left*, or the ones *opposite*. It is not necessary to apply fusible webbing to appliqué fabrics for hand appliqué.
   Note: For easier handling, the top is appliquéd in three sections. Each of these three sections is first basted together for marking and then taken apart.

Cutting the fabrics
From the checked fabric, cut one 32x92-inch center section and two 20½x92-inch side sections.
   From each of the three green fabrics, set aside ⅝ yard for the tulip stems. Use the rest of the green fabric for the leaves, following the instructions for preparing the appliqués.

Preparing the quilt top
Using ½-inch seams, machine-baste one side section to each long edge of the center section.

Using a fabric marker, draw a 67x88-inch rectangle on the quilt top to mark the finished size. There should be a 2-inch fabric allowance around all edges.

Draw another rectangle 3 inches *inside* the 67x88-inch rectangle to mark the leaf placement.

Preparing the appliqué patterns
The size of the tulip appliqué patterns prevents us from giving a complete full-size pattern in this book. We have provided both a gridded pattern and a full-size pattern for one tulip and leaf to assist those who wish to draw their tulip garden freehand.

For marking the quilt top, draw the outlines of the leaves, stems, and tulips in dark lines. Lightly color leaves and stems in varying shades of green and the tulips in colors that match your fabrics.

ENLARGING THE TULIP GARDEN PATTERN: Opaque projectors are available in many public libraries or school media centers. Slide the gridded pattern into the projector, and it will transfer the image onto a wall. Tape paper onto the wall and trace the pattern outlines with a pencil.

A print shop can enlarge the patterns and make a photostatic copy. This is a quick process (often while you wait), but it can be expensive. Ask for a cost estimate beforehand.

The gridded pattern, *opposite*, is in two sections—a pink center motif and a gray corner. If you want to alter the finished size of the quilt, add or subtract from the center motif at the sides as necessary to achieve the desired size.

Enlarge the pattern to scale. The corner motif measures about 16⅝x22½ inches. The length of the center motif is approximately 29⅝ inches; the tulips vary from 4 inches to 14 inches in height. Leaf A is 12 inches high.

DRAWING TULIPS FREEHAND: These leaf and tulip shapes are simple to draw. We have provided one full-size leaf and the generic flower shape to get you started.
continued

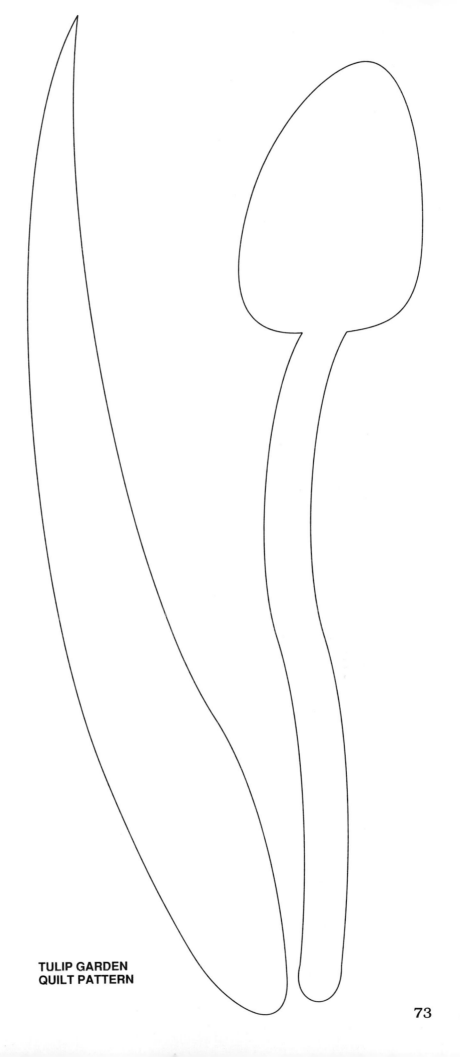

**TULIP GARDEN
QUILT PATTERN**

Using the gridded pattern as a guide, draw a tulip garden that matches the dimensions stated on the previous page. The leaves and stems can be any shape you like, and variety will add interest to your garden. Vary the length of the stems to make the garden appear lifelike.

Marking the quilt top

If you can see the outlines of the drawn shapes through the fabric, you can work on any flat surface. If not, tape the pattern onto a window so the sunlight makes the pattern visible through the fabric.

Fit the corner motif into one corner of the quilt top, aligning the leaf bottoms with the inner rectangle drawn on the quilt top.

To extend the side motif across the short end of the quilt top, overlap the A leaves on the quilt top and on the pattern, and continue marking.

Continue rotating and transferring the pattern around the quilt, aligning A leaves each time.

When the pattern is marked around the entire quilt top, remove the basted seams so the appliqué can be worked on three separate sections.

Preparing the appliqué fabrics

MACHINE APPLIQUÉ: Trace all the leaf, stem, and tulip shapes from your pattern onto the paper side of the fusible webbing. Follow the manufacturer's instructions to fuse the webbing to the wrong sides of the appropriate fabrics. Cut out all the shapes.

HAND APPLIQUÉ: Trace all the leaf and tulip shapes from the pattern directly onto the appliqué fabrics. Cut out each shape, adding a 3/16-inch seam allowance.

For the tulip stems, cut 120 inches of 1¼-inch-wide continuous bias from each of the three green fabrics. (Refer to tips on making continuous bias on page 79.) Handle the bias carefully to avoid stretching it.

With right sides together, stitch the raw edges of the bias together in a ¼-inch seam. Trim the seam allowance slightly, then turn the tube right side out. Press the bias strip flat, with the seam line in the center back.

Cut strips of bias to match the stem lengths.

Appliquéing the quilt top

MACHINE APPLIQUÉ: Set the sewing machine to make a tight, narrow zigzag stitch. Experiment with scrap fabrics to find the best setting for your machine; practice making points and curves.

You may find machine appliqué easier if you place typing or tracing paper under the quilt top as you stitch. As you sew through all layers, the paper acts as a stabilizer and keeps the fabric from shifting and stretching. Tear the paper away when the stitching is complete.

Fuse all leaves onto the quilt top *except* those that fall across the seams.

Stitch around the outer edges of each leaf, using a matching thread for each fabric.

Fuse and sew all the stems in place in the same manner as for the leaves. Appliqué the tulips onto the quilt last.

HAND APPLIQUÉ: Turn under the edges of the appliqué pieces. Pin or baste each leaf in position on the quilt top.

Using a tiny, hidden slip stitch, appliqué the leaves in place, then the stems and tulips. It is not necessary to sew down an edge that will be covered by another piece.

Assembling the quilt top

Sew the quilt sections back together, then appliqué the leaves, stems, and tulips that lie over the seam lines.

Using a ruler and a nonpermanent marker, draw a grid of quilting lines across the center of the quilt top. The quilt pictured on pages 66 and 67 has 4½-inch squares marked seven squares across and 11 down.

Quilting and finishing

Cut the backing fabric into two 2¾-yard lengths; seam the pieces together. Cut the backing and the batting down to the same size as the quilt top.

Layer the backing, batting, and quilt top. Baste all layers horizontally, vertically, and diagonally. Baste along the outside of quilt.

Quilt by hand or by machine along the marked lines, stitching through all layers. Quilt along one edge of all stems that do not overlap leaves and around the tulip heads. Add additional quilting as desired. Remove basting.

Trim excess batting, backing, and quilt top to ½ inch past the finished quilt outline. Baste edges together around the quilt.

Make 9½ yards of 3-inch-wide binding (see page 79 for tips on making and applying binding). Sew binding around quilt edges, taking a ½-inch seam allowance.

Pillow Ticking Quilt

Shown on page 68.

The finished quilt measures approximately 64x92 inches.

MATERIALS

4¼ yards of 32-inch-wide pillow ticking or 3½ yards of 44-inch-wide striped fabric
2¼ yards of teal fabric for borders
¼ yard of purple fabric for border corners
5⅝ yards of backing fabric
81x96-inch quilt batting
Rotary cutter, mat, and ruler
260 assorted buttons

INSTRUCTIONS

A practical alternative to using buttons is to tie the quilt with multicolored scraps of pearl cotton or embroidery floss.

Cutting the fabrics

Cut the ticking or striped fabric into 4½-inch-wide strips, cutting across the width of the fabric. Cut each strip into 4½-inch squares until you have 228 squares.

From the teal border fabric, cut two strips 8½x78 inches and two strips 8½x48½ inches.

Cut four 8½-inch squares of purple fabric for border corners.

Assembling the quilt

Sew 12 ticking squares together to form a row, alternating the direction of the stripes with each piece. (See photograph on page 68 for reference.) Press the seam allowances in one direction.

Repeat to make 18 more rows, making sure that nine strips start and end with horizontal stripes and the remainder start and end with vertical stripes.

Stitch the rows together, alternating rows of horizontal and vertical stripes. Press the seam allowances to one side.

Sew a 78-inch-long border strip onto each long side of the quilt. Trim excess border fabric even with the quilt top at each end.

Sew a purple square to each end of the remaining teal pieces; sew borders to top and bottom of quilt, matching seam lines of corners with side border seams.

Finishing

Cut the backing fabric into two 96-inch lengths. Sew these two pieces together into one panel of approximately 70x96 inches.

Baste the batting securely to the wrong side of the quilt top, working outward from the center horizontally, vertically, and diagonally. Baste around the edges. Trim batting even with quilt top.

Pin the quilt top to the backing fabric with right sides together. Machine-stitch around all edges, leaving a 9-inch opening in one side for turning. Trim the seams; turn right side out and stitch the opening closed.

Sew buttons at all intersections of the ticking squares, stitching through all layers. If desired, add more buttons on the teal borders.

Stars and Stripes Quilt

Shown on page 69.

The finished quilt measures approximately 72x94 inches.

MATERIALS

¼ yard *each* of 25 assorted solid fabrics, a total of 6¼ yards
1¾ yards of cranberry solid fabric for outer border
¾ yard of black solid fabric for inner border
¾ yard of black star print fabric for binding
5½ yards of backing fabric
81x96-inch precut quilt batting
Acrylic ruler
Rotary cutter and mat

INSTRUCTIONS

The 28 vertical strips of this quilt are made with random lengths of different solid fabrics. When sewn together, the strips create a pattern of color. The more random the piecing, the more interesting the finished quilt will be.

We used a dark fabric with a large star print for the binding. This adds a nice touch of pattern to the solid fabrics of the quilt top.

These instructions are for a twin-size bed quilt. Length and width are easily adjusted to fit a larger bed by adding strips.

Cutting the fabrics

From each ¼-yard piece of solid-colored fabric, cut three 2½-inch-wide strips. Cut cross grain, from selvage to selvage.

Cut these strips into random lengths, ranging from 6 inches to 18 inches long.

For the inner border, cut nine 2½-inch-wide strips of the black solid fabric. Cut cross grain.

Cut the cranberry border fabric in the same manner, cutting nine 6-inch-wide strips.

Assembling the quilt top

To piece each vertical strip, randomly select fabrics of different colors and lengths. Sew fabric pieces end to end until the strip is at least 78 inches long.

Make 28 vertical strips. Press seam allowances in one direction.

Sew the rows together in four groups of seven rows each, then join the four units to complete the quilt top. Press seams.

Square off the top and bottom edges of the quilt if the strips are of unequal lengths. The assembled quilt top should measure approximately 56½x78 inches.

Adding the borders

Sew two black border strips end to end for the top and bottom borders. Matching the center seam of the border with the center of the quilt, stitch borders to the top and bottom edges of the quilt top.

Press seam allowance toward the black fabric; trim excess border fabric at quilt sides.

Seam three black border strips for each of the side borders. Sew side borders onto quilt top in the same manner.

Join the cranberry fabric strips in the same manner for the outer border. Sew border strips onto quilt top, sewing top and bottom edges first, then the side edges.

Quilting and finishing

Divide the backing fabric into two 99-inch-long panels. Remove the selvages, then seam the pieces together. Press the seam allowance to one side.

Layer backing fabric, batting, and quilt top. Baste all layers securely together.

The quilt pictured on page 69 is quilted in an all-over clamshell pattern. Quilt as desired.

Use the star print fabric to make approximately 340 inches of 2½-inch-wide binding, either bias or straight grain. Refer to page 79 for tips on making and applying binding.

Pony Express Star Quilt

Shown on pages 70 and 71.

The finished quilt measures approximately 68x92 inches. Each star block is 12 inches square.

MATERIALS

2½ yards of light tan print fabric for star background
2¼ yards of brown print fabric for outer border and binding
⅜ yard of green print fabric for inner border
⅛ yard to ¼ yard *each* of at least 31 assorted print fabrics, a total of 4 yards
5½ yards of backing fabric
81x96-inch precut quilt batting
Acrylic ruler
Rotary cutter and mat

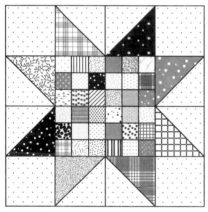

PONY EXPRESS STAR

INSTRUCTIONS

The secret to this quilt's success is the use of a wide variety of fabric prints and colors. Tan, brown, green, red, dark blue, light blue, and deep rose are randomly scattered throughout the squares and triangles of the 24 stars and surrounding borders. Use a mix of light, medium, and dark fabrics and small- and medium-scale prints, stripes, and plaids.

Cutting the fabrics

Note: Cut fabrics in strips, using a rotary cutter and an acrylic ruler for accurate cutting. Cut all strips cross grain, selvage to selvage, then cut the strips down into the required squares and triangles.

From the tan background fabric, cut eight 3½x42-inch strips.

Cut twelve 3½-inch squares from each strip, a total of 96, for the corner squares of the star block.

Cut the remaining tan fabric into ten 3⅞x42-inch strips. Cut ten 3⅞-inch squares from each strip, then cut each square in half *diagonally* to obtain a total of 200 triangles. This includes eight more triangles than are needed for this quilt; set the extras aside.

Cut eight 6-inch-wide strips of the brown print fabric for the outer borders. Set aside the remaining fabric for the binding.

For the inner border, cut eight 1½-inch-wide strips of the green print fabric. Add the remaining green print fabric to the assorted prints for the star patchwork.

From *each* of the assorted print fabrics, cut a 1½x42-inch strip. Cut each strip into twenty-eight 1½-inch squares—a total of 868.

Cut 180 squares from the remaining prints, each 3⅞ inches square. Cut each square in half *diagonally* to make 360 triangles for stars and the pieced border.

Piecing the star block

Select 36 squares for the center of each block, choosing a random assortment of colors and prints.

Sew the squares together, making small units that can be joined to complete the center square. Start by making three rows of three squares each; press all the seam allowances in one direction.

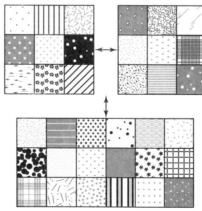

FIGURE 1

Stitch three rows together in a nine-patch square, turning the rows as necessary to alternate the direction of the seam allowances. Join four nine-patches to complete the center square as illustrated in Figure 1, *above.*

Select eight different print triangles for the star points. Join each print triangle with one triangle of tan fabric, making eight triangle-squares.

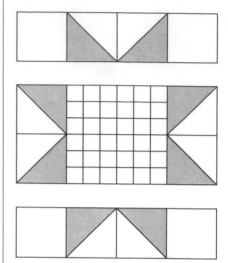

BLOCK ASSEMBLY DIAGRAM

Stitch the triangle-squares together into four pairs, matching the right sides and raw edges of the tan triangles. Press the seam allowances to one side.

Referring to the Block Assembly Diagram, *above,* join a pair of star points to opposite sides of the center square, positioning the tan triangles to the outside of the block. Press the seam allowances toward the triangles.

Stitch a square of tan background fabric onto both ends of the two remaining triangle units. Press the seam allowances toward the dark triangles. Complete the block by joining these pieced units to the top and bottom edges of the center unit as shown in the assembly diagram.

Make 24 Pony Express Star blocks. Each block should measure 12½ inches.

Assembling the blocks

Aligning the matching seam lines carefully, sew four blocks together in a row. Press the seam allowances to one side.

Make six rows, with four star blocks in each row. Stitch the rows together to complete the quilt top, referring to the quilt diagram, *opposite.*

Adding the triangle border

Join random pairs of the remaining print triangles to make 84 triangle-squares.

Select 16 squares for the top border. Assemble the squares in a row, randomly positioning the direction of the diagonal seams as shown in the quilt drawing at *right*. Press the seam allowances in one direction. Make a 16-square border for the bottom edge in the same manner.

Stitch 26 triangle-squares together for *each* side border.

Sew top and bottom borders onto the quilt top first, then add the side borders. Press seam allowances toward the borders.

Adding the remaining borders

Seam two strips of dark green fabric end to end to obtain a border strip long enough for each side of the quilt. Make four border strips; press seam allowances to one side.

Stitch one border strip to the top edge of the quilt, matching the centers of the border and the quilt top. Repeat for the bottom edge. Press the seam allowances toward the green border, then trim excess border fabric.

Add side borders of the dark green fabric in the same manner.

Join pairs of brown print border strips and add borders in the same manner as for the green print borders, sewing the top and bottom borders to the quilt first, then the side borders.

Quilting and finishing

Divide the backing fabric into two 2¾-yard-long panels. Remove the selvages, then seam the pieces together. Press the seam allowance to one side.

Layer backing fabric, batting, and quilt top. Baste all layers securely together.

The quilt shown is quilted in the "ditch" (seam lines) of all the triangle-squares, with a simple cross-hatching of 1½-inch diagonal squares quilted in the wide border. Quilt as desired.

Refer to page 79 for tips on how to make and apply binding. Use the remaining brown print fabric to make approximately 330 inches of 2½-inch-wide binding, either bias or straight grain.

PONY EXPRESS STAR QUILT

Washing Your Quilt

Any quilt that is used eventually needs cleaning. Some people have enough faith in today's strong, durable fabrics to toss quilts in the washing machine and dryer. Others wash them gently by hand in a large tub or wading pool.

Antique quilts should be handled with extreme care. Seek expert advice before you attempt to clean an antique.

The following tips help ensure that the quilt you make will survive an occasional washing with flying colors.

● Prewash all fabrics, including the backing. Wash the fabric in whatever way you intend to clean the finished quilt, whether that means washing it in the machine or by hand. Press the fabric carefully before cutting it.

● Use a washable batting. Most bonded polyester batts wash well.

● Always use a mild soap; never use bleach. A heavily soiled quilt may require extra soaking.

● Dry a wet quilt by laying it flat on the floor or outside on an overcast day (bright sun causes fabric colors to fade). Wet fabric is very heavy, so avoid hanging or lifting the quilt in a way that puts stress on the fabric or seams. Air a musty quilt in the same manner.

● Dry cleaning is not advisable.

Using Templates To Mark Fabric

A template is a duplication of a printed pattern that is traced onto fabric to define the piece to be cut.

Although straight-sided shapes can be marked onto the fabric with a ruler, it is necessary to use a template to trace other shapes. Templates are most widely used to mark sewing lines for hand piecing and appliqué.

Making a template

You can make a template by gluing a traced paper pattern onto cardboard or sandpaper, but these materials are difficult to cut and will fray with repeated use.

We recommend template plastic, available at most crafts supply stores. It is lightweight, making it easy to cut with scissors or an art knife. Plastic can be used many times because it does not fray.

The transparency of plastic offers additional advantages. When transparent plastic is placed atop a printed page, the pattern is visible and easily traced onto its surface without intermediate steps.

Trace the pattern onto your chosen template material. Always use a ruler to draw true lines and corners on the material. Cut out the template on the drawn lines.

Label each template with its letter designation, the block name, and the grain line indicated on the pattern. Verify the template's size by placing it over the printed pattern. Templates must be accurate, or the error, however small, will be compounded many times as the quilt is assembled.

Using a template

To mark the fabric, use a pencil, chalk, or other marker that draws a thin, clear line. Do not use ballpoint or ink pens; the ink may bleed when the fabric is washed.

Position the grain line marked on the template parallel to the fabric grain. Always place curved edges on the bias. Trace around the template onto the fabric. Cut each piece on the drawn lines.

To check the accuracy of your templates and marking, make a test block before cutting out the rest of the quilt pieces.

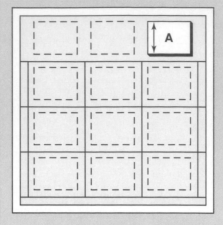

1 For hand piecing, templates are usually cut to the exact *finished* size of the patch, without seam allowances added. Place the template *facedown* on the *wrong* side of the fabric; position the tracings at least ½ inch apart. These marked lines are *sewing lines.* Some quilters mark cutting lines as well, but experienced quilters cut the pieces apart by eye, adding a ¼-inch seam allowance around each piece.

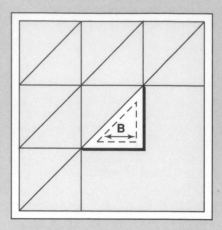

2 For machine piecing, make a template with the seam allowances included. This enables you to mark pieces using common lines for efficient cutting. Place the templates *facedown* on the *wrong* side of the fabric, and mark around them. Using sharp scissors or a rotary cutter, cut exactly on the drawn lines.

3 A window template can be used for hand or machine patchwork. By drawing both the cutting and sewing lines, precision is enhanced for both methods. Having a drawn seam line is especially useful as guidance for set-in pieces by machine, where pivoting at a precise point is critical. When used on the right side of the fabric, window templates also enable you to cut out specific fabric motifs with accuracy.

4 Templates for hand appliqué are made the *finished* size. Place these templates *faceup* on the *right* side of the fabric. Position tracings ½ inch apart. Cut out each shape, adding a ³⁄₁₆-inch seam allowance around each piece. The drawn line provides a guideline for turning under the seam allowance for sewing.

How to Make and Apply Binding

There are several ways to bind the edges of a finished quilt. Most require extra fabric to make a separate binding strip.

These instructions are for a French-fold, or doubled, binding, which is more durable than the traditional single layer.

Yardage for binding is listed for each project in this book; it is sufficient to make French-fold binding cut 2½ inches wide on either the bias or straight of the grain.

The binding fabric should be prewashed in the same manner as the other quilt fabrics.

Making straight-grain binding

One way to make straight binding is to cut lengthwise strips, each 2 to 3 inches longer than the quilt edge to be bound. Make square corners as described here.

To make a continuous strip of straight-grain binding, piece the cut strips end to end. Press these seams open to distribute the bulk of the seam allowance.

Making continuous bias binding

Referring to Figure 1, *far right,* draw a diagonal line from the bottom corner to the top edge. Use a plastic triangle to draw accurate 45-degree angles. Cut the fabric on the drawn line.

Matching their straight edges, sew the two fabric pieces together with a ¼-inch seam allowance as shown in Figure 2, *far right.* Press the seam allowance open.

Use a pencil or marker with a ruler to draw parallel lines across the length of the seamed fabric. The space between lines is the desired width of the binding strip, including seam allowances. Cutting strips 2 to 2½ inches wide results in a finished quilt binding of approximately ⅜ inch.

Bring the diagonal edges together, right sides facing, to create a tube of fabric. Shift one edge down so that it aligns with the first marked line of the opposite edge as shown in Figure 3, *far right.* The other end also is offset.

Holding the fabric in position, stitch the two edges together; press the seam open. Handle the fabric gently to avoid stretching the bias.

Start cutting at one uneven end along the marked line. Each time you cut across the seam, you'll be moving down one marked line, cutting a continuous spiral.

Applying binding

The quilt should be quilted and securely basted around the edges before binding is applied.

Bring the raw edges of the binding strip together, folding the fabric in half lengthwise with the wrong sides together. Sew the raw edges of the binding strip to the quilt edge as described below.

SQUARE CORNERS: Sew binding onto two opposite sides of the quilt, from corner to corner. Trim batting and backing to a ⅜-inch seam allowance.

Fold binding over edge; hand-stitch in place on the backing. Trim excess fabric at each end.

Sew binding onto the remaining quilt sides, overlapping the first bound edges. Trim excess fabric, leaving about ¼ inch extra on both ends of the side.

Fold this extra fabric over the first binding as shown in Figure 4, *right.* Then fold the binding strip over the quilt edge to the back, enclosing all the raw edges (Figure 5, *right*). Hand-sew the binding in place.

MITERED CORNERS: A continuous binding strip is needed to make folded mitered corners.

Match raw edges of binding and quilt top at the center of any side. Turn under ½ inch of binding.

Stitch ¼ inch from the edge, sewing through all layers. Stop stitching ¼ inch from the corner.

Fold the binding straight up, away from the corner (Figure 6, *right*). Then bring the binding down, in line with the adjacent side as shown in Figure 7, *right.* Begin stitching the next side at the top fold of the binding, sewing through all layers.

Stitch around the quilt in this manner. At the starting point, overlap the binding beyond the first fold (Figure 8, *right*). When the binding is turned over the edge to the back, the fold in the binding covers the raw edge.

Trim excess batting and backing to a ⅜-inch seam allowance. Turn the binding over the edge to the back of the quilt. Hand-stitch the binding in place.

To finish the miters on the quilt back, hand-stitch right up to the corner and then fold the binding over the next side (figures 9 and 10, *below*). Tack a stitch or two in the miter fold to secure it, then proceed along the next edge.

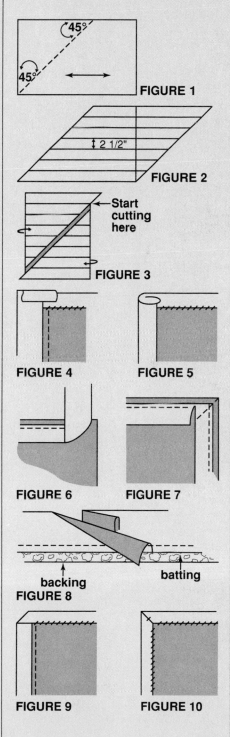

FIGURE 1

FIGURE 2

FIGURE 3

FIGURE 4

FIGURE 5

FIGURE 6

FIGURE 7

FIGURE 8

FIGURE 9

FIGURE 10

ACKNOWLEDGMENTS

We would like to extend our thanks to the following designers who contributed projects to this book.

Linda Beardsley—68

Marianne Fons—52

Marilyn Ginsburg—54–55; 70–71

Julie Hart—37

Lynette Jensen—4–5, 50–51; 69

Janice Karaba—22–23, farm

Anne MacKinnon—34

Mimi Schimm—7

Margaret Sindelar—53

Patricia Wilens—8–9; 35

Jim Williams—22–23, quilt; 66–67

Jo Wilson—36

We would like to thank the following people, whose technical skills are greatly appreciated.

Sue Bahr

Esther Grischkowsky

Julie Hart

Lynette Jensen

Margaret Sindelar

Judy Veeder

Evalee Waltz

We extend a special thank-you to the following people who graciously loaned us antiques or otherwise assisted in the production of this book.

Pam and Harry Bookey

Lynda and David Haupert

Theresa Lemrick

Diane and Cal Lewis

Donna and Robert Martin

Sue and Mark Pennington

For their cooperation and courtesy, we extend a special thanks to the following sources:

Hoffman of California
25792 Obrero Rd.
Mission Viejo, CA 92691
    for the puzzle fabric on
        pages 4–5
    for the sky fabric on
        pages 50–51

Waverly
79 Madison Ave.
New York, NY 10016
    for purple checked fabric on
        pages 50–51
    (Fabric No. 657072)

We also are pleased to acknowledge the following photographers whose talents and technical skills contributed much to this book.

Perry Struse—34

WM. Hopkins, Hopkins Associates—all other photos